REVOLUTION ROAD TRIP

REVOLUTION ROAD TRIP

**Our Two Wild and World-Changing Weeks
behind the Iron Curtain**

KELLY KIMBALL TRISH WHITCOMB
ANDREW FRANK BARRY FADEM

LIONCREST
PUBLISHING

REVOLUTION ROAD TRIP
Our Two Wild and World-Changing Weeks behind the Iron Curtain

FIRST EDITION

ISBN   978-1-5445-2906-6   *Hardcover*
       978-1-5445-2905-9   *Paperback*
       978-1-5445-2907-3   *Ebook*
       978-1-5445-4343-7   *Audiobook*

This book is dedicated to Dr. J. Phillips Noble. What he stood for in life was fairness, equality, and democracy. These principles inspired us to write this book but, more importantly, should inspire young people around the world to defend and endorse democracy, especially in these fragile times.

CONTENTS

INTRODUCTION

WE NEVER MEANT TO BREAK UP A COUNTRY.

It was only a short trip to support the elections in Eastern Europe in 1990. We went to give general political advice to new democrats—small "d"—and to have a wild time. But while we gave our seminars and speeches, and while we did have a wild time, something else happened, too.

We inadvertently ended up advising a particular party in a particular part of Europe whose election would, for better or for worse, mark a turning point in the lives of millions of people.

Really, we were mainly there out of curiosity to see this novel world that had only just opened up to outsiders after the fall of communism in the Soviet Union and across the Eastern Bloc. And to have a wild time. We drank a lot of Czech beer (very good), Hungarian wine (good), and Russian champagne (less so). We talked a lot, often after copious amounts of Czech beer (insightful), Hungarian wine (moderately insightful), and Russian champagne (gibberish).

More importantly, we also encountered the kind of participatory democracy that none of us had ever seen before and most of us haven't witnessed again since.

This was politics as *politics*: not the world-weary trudge or reluctant drive to the polling station, not gathering signatures on ballot propositions in shopping malls, not sending postcards to registered voters who possibly couldn't even remember why they belonged to a party in the first place. This was the kind of politics that meant something. That inspired the Athenians to climb the hill to the Pnyx to vote. That inspired the Suffragists to face jail or death to win the right to vote. That inspired the Selma marchers to stand their ground in the face of police attacking them with tear gas and charging horsemen on the Edmund Pettus Bridge. That inspires millions of voters to wait hours in line to cast their ballot from Kabul to Johannesburg, El Savador, Algeria, Liberia, and even some places in the United States.

Hell, you've got to love *that* sort of politics. *We* loved that sort of politics. Though looking back through the lens of everything that has happened since in Eastern European politics, US politics, and global politics, it feels as if we were in a different world. For sure, we were different people then.

So that's how we'll write our story: as if it was something that happened to other people. Of course, this was all thirty years ago, so our recollections aren't necessarily perfect, nor are those of the others who were on that same journey to whom we've reached out. We think it's all accurate, more or less, and if it's a little embellished here or words are attributed to the wrong person there, or we inadvertently cause mild embarrassment to individuals, then do believe us that any such shortcomings are accidental rather than malevolent. Put it this way: we've tried to get it as right as we can just because that's the best way to tell the story.

All of this is meant to say that we hope our story will give you an idea of what we did in a past life that will make you smile a little, learn a little, and not reach for a computer to send us angry emails.

UNINTENDED CONSEQUENCES

They only wanted to help. They were only there for a couple of weeks. There were only a couple dozen—maybe a few more—back-of-house political operators from the United States, Canada, South America, and all over. Kelly Kimball and Barry Fadem worked on ballot initiatives in numerous states throughout the US; Trish Whitcomb was a direct-mail specialist; Andrew Frank was a campaign advance man.

They were all on a whistle-stop tour to help new parties understand how to compete and win in the first free elections in Eastern Europe in decades. Like a school trip but with seminars.

What harm could they do?

Other than losing Barry Fadem's glasses, followed by losing Fadem himself. And offending a roomful of Hungarians (Kimball still blames an interpreter's SNAFU). And outraging a bunch of staunchly Catholic Poles when Kimball decided to promote reproductive rights. And upsetting the American Embassy in Prague that a bunch of folks they'd never heard of were apparently helping fight an election down in Bratislava, the capital of Slovakia.

Though probably not upsetting them as much as the Czech minister for buses.

Of course, it's a truth universally acknowledged, to paraphrase Jane Austen, that politics in the United States is held in low repute; that most politicians are held in even lower repute;

and that the lowest levels of public opinion are reserved for the campaigners, managers, policy-makers, and fixers who get the politicians elected and help them govern.

"Hacks," according to their critics. The foot soldiers of democracy, to their supporters. A pain in the ass, according to the American embassy in Prague. And the Czech minister for buses.

But not, in this case, the people who did the damage.

They did help, in a small way, the Slovaks elect candidates running under the banner of Public Against Violence (Verejnosť Proti Násiliu -VPN), some individuals among whom would eventually lead them out of their federation with the Czechs to create their own country. That's true. Czechoslovakia broke into Slovakia on one side and the Czech Republic on the other. But that was four years after the North Americans were there, and it was never their intention, nor the overt intention of anyone who worked with them.

Even amid the chaotic politics of Eastern Europe in the years after the fall of the Berlin Wall and the Soviet Union, what was happening in Czechoslovakia stood out to the outside observer as something random, an accident.

Call it the law of unintended consequences or Murphy's Law. An unexpected scandal just two days before the election, an accidental candidate, a nationalistic economic policy— and a world diverted by other, larger events than what was happening in Bratislava. The first elections in the reunified Germany; elections in other, larger and more familiar countries from the former Soviet bloc; even elections in Prague, in the "Czech" part of Czechoslovakia, made sure Bratislava got nowhere near the front pages of the international newspapers or onto TV screens in many places other than Slovakia itself.

Even those people who *were* taking any notice of what was

happening in Czechoslovakia rarely looked past Václav Havel, the playwright who was appointed president in early 1990 and officially elected to the post in June. Or possibly Alexander Dubček, who dazzled the world when he stood up to Soviet rule during the Prague Spring of 1968 but was now living quietly out of public life, working for the forestry service.

Even the political professionals arriving for campaign technology seminars didn't notice any signs that hinted that Slovakia would become independent, and those folks were actually there. On the ground.

It wasn't part of their story. And they weren't part of *that* story. That story was the culmination of a chain of events that had left the station long before they got there.

The divisions within the country had been there for a long time. While the Czech and Slovak languages are very similar and both can understand each other—the TV channels used both—the Czechs were always considered the more cultured part of the population. The Slovaks, meanwhile, were a more industrial and agrarian society in some ways closer to their neighbors to the east than the Czechs, who in turn were closer to their neighbors to the west. Prague was widely seen as the "Paris of Eastern Europe," while Slovakia was more similar to its eastern European neighbors in history and culture.

In the beginning, the political consultants weren't there to win an election.

Strictly speaking, they weren't even meant to visit Slovakia at all. The original itinerary of the trip included only Budapest in Hungary, Prague in Czechoslovakia, and Warsaw in Poland. Like a trunk show, they were meant to roll into town, set up shop, and give a series of workshops over a couple of days to anyone interested in finding out about promoting candidates, sharpening messages, or getting out the vote.

In other words, they would be talking about skills that had not been in much demand in Eastern Europe for decades—not since the Iron Curtain came down—that had suddenly become highly popular.

These were countries where virtually no one knew anything about running a campaign for a democratic election. They'd been under effective one-party rule by the Communists for four decades. People from the Western world who thought they knew it all about democracy—Americans, Brits, Europeans—rushed to give the parties that were emerging their best advice. The National Democratic Institute and the International Republican Institute sent people to Budapest, Prague, and Warsaw (and Moscow and Berlin). The German Christian Democrats and German Social Democrats had people on the ground. France set up academies and sent cultural ambassadors to countries across the region. Everyone wanted to get in the game.

No one rushed to Bratislava. Most of the advisors who descended on Eastern Europe early in 1990 would have been hard-placed to point it out on a map or to explain the historical relationship between the Slovaks and the Czechs.

Let's face it: neither could most of the consultants on the tour.

Their presence was serendipity. It was the result of a chance conversation between the field manager of the trip, Andrew Frank, with some folks in Prague who worked for Civic Forum, which was the umbrella group for the coalition that was formed by and supported Václav Havel. Someone casually mentioned that their sister party in Slovakia, VPN, might like to hear what the visitors were saying about how to participate in democratic politics.

That led to another conversation between Frank and the

group that originally sent the visitors out behind the Iron Curtain, *Campaigns & Elections* (C&E) in Washington, DC, publishers of *the* trade magazine for political consultants. There were no cell phones, only landlines and fax machines, so Frank called back to Jennifer Laszlo Mizrahi, his main contact at C&E, and explained what he had been told. He thought it sounded like a good idea, he told her. Mizrahi had to check with her bosses—the publisher James Dwinell and Scott Berkowitz—and she wasn't sure she could sell it to the traveling party. Their attention had been grabbed by the thought of cultural centers like Budapest and Prague, not Bratislava.

Frank faxed over a letter of invitation and said he was going on to Warsaw, so there were a few days before he would make it to Bratislava to check it out—if C&E thought that was a good idea. C&E had created a lucrative sideline to the magazine by organizing similar types of seminars in a number of parts of the world. They could sniff an opportunity.

Ultimately, Mizrahi got the green light. Sure, she said, go to Bratislava.

So they went.

What Andrew, Barry, Kelly, Trish, and others did there probably didn't change much for the Slovaks, although they did, in a very small way, support VPN's victory in the regional general election. Or, to be more precise, Frank did. By then, the others were back home, offering advice and financial support—and a few computers that would have been helpful if they'd gotten there quicker.

For all anyone knows, some of those computers might still be stuck in customs at the Austrian border, buried under decades of red tape and yellowing paperwork. The others were only retrieved when Frank and some VPN people drove up to the border to release them from Austrian customs.

But if the US consultants didn't manage to change the course of Slovak history, they did change their own histories. They saw democracy up close, struggling to establish itself—and they looked on in awe as they saw a people's yearning for freedom struggle to bring a democratic country into existence, despite having few traditions, precedents, or systems to base it upon, and no guarantee it would succeed.

They encountered excitement from some people, fear from others, and ambivalence from yet more. The key drivers calling for change in all the countries they visited were a combination of seasoned activists—Lech Walesa and Solidarnosc in Poland, Charter 77 in Czechoslovakia, and others—along with young people (aged about eighteen to thirty) who wanted change and forge a new future for themselves. Often they disagreed about the way ahead with parents who were far more familiar with and comfortable in the communist system. These were people who only knew what democracy looks like by observing it from afar, reading about it in books, and watching it on TV shows from the West, but were now trying to create it for themselves. It was a bit like trying to build a car based on seeing one drive by.

That was way back near the start of the Americans' careers, in the early 1990s. They were young and idealistic but already jaded from the years they'd spent in US politics: jaded from slick operations, instant polls, focus groups, changeable politicians, fickle voters, snake oil salesmen, unfulfillable promises, buried scandals, interest groups, thwarted elections.

Now, they found themselves sitting in rooms with people who had been sent to prison for dreaming of free and fair elections. With a person who had been imprisoned for nothing more than possessing a book, not even for reading it. It was like nothing they'd ever encountered before or since—and yet it was also exactly why they had all gotten into politics in the first place.

They all believed that democracy could improve the lives of everyone. And even though the American system had so far largely failed to live up to such a romantic notion of politics, for just about the first time in their lives, they were in the right place at the right time to be able to help.

It was a game of politics with stakes and hazards the likes of which they had never come across in their professional lives.

The US democratic system was well over 200 years old; Czechoslovakia's was a few months old (the Velvet Revolution that ended Communist rule had happened in December 1989). As far as the Americans were concerned, whatever expertise they had, any of the people they met were welcome to it.

At the time, Eastern Europe was flooded by US political advisors eager to play midwife to the nascent democracies, but most of them had been drawn to higher-profile places such as Prague or Budapest (higher profile meaning that most Americans had actually heard of them). Some of the biggest stars in the firmament of US election advisors were on the ground in those cities, competing to influence the generation of new politicians who were going to shape post-Communist Europe.

Few political operatives from North America had thought to head to Bratislava, so there wasn't that much competition there. In terms of any significant presence, the C&E group was the only game in town.

That's how they came to be involved in a small election a long way from home. It's not an episode that many Americans know much about—or many Europeans, for that matter. In the context of the end of the Cold War, the defeat of Communism, the fall of the Iron Curtain, and the Berlin Wall, it escaped most people's attention. It was never much more than a footnote. All this time later, it might only be a footnote to a footnote.

But it mattered. It mattered to the Slovaks. And ultimately, it mattered to the young advisors.

And it's a story worth telling, even if it is incomplete all this time later, and details have become lost or confused with the passage of time. Unless it's written down, it'll be as if it never happened.

Many of the people who led the revolution in Slovakia in 1989 have died or are now in their sixties or seventies; the American visitors are, too. Even though they only know a tiny part of the story—and even though they were on the outside looking in—it's still a good story.

People in Eastern Europe were giddy with the excitement of freedom. The visitors from North America saw the same thing in Hungary, Czechoslovakia, and Poland. There were posters everywhere aimed at the departing Soviets, most of which were variations on the theme of "Don't let the door hit you on the ass on your way out."

But there were divisions, too. The communists might have gone, but the autocratic governments were soon replaced by squabbling, fractious parties and factions. For every person who wanted to rush to embrace liberal democracy, there was another who felt more comfortable remaining closer to the communist model. Each country was at a different stage of the transition, and the nuances were fascinating. Even within VPN, there were differences and tensions that would eventually break the movement apart.

It didn't help that Ján Budaj, who led the Velvet Revolution in Slovakia, was exposed two days before the election as having been an informer for the secret police. His publication of a scathing essay on environmental conditions in Czechoslovakia had resulted in threats to the personal safety of his family, and it was alleged his solution to securing their protection was to collaborate with the Communists while he was secreted away for an extended period of time in the 1970s.

Whatever the reason behind his decision, that was a bad look for a party standing against everything associated with the communists. Budaj quit, and his departure opened the way for more aggressive nationalists to gain power in the VPN.

Many of those who led the revolution in Slovakia soon found themselves sidelined. They were the idealists, dissidents, campaigners, economists, and theorists: people who were better at thinking and articulating, proposing, and debating than they were at politics.

In fact, part of the advisors' role was to introduce them to the idea that politics isn't some rarified higher pursuit: it's a grind of practicalities, compromise, drudgery, maneuvering constant challenges, and failures.

And it's a lot harder when there isn't a common enemy to fight against, like communism.

When their colleague Juraj Mihalik of the VPN wrote a book looking back at the election and at how the promise of VPN's victory turned sour, he called it *Velvet Failures*.

It was in Juraj's apartment in the Old Town of Bratislava one memorable evening—well, a largely forgotten memorable evening, given the beer and wine—that their involvement with Slovakian politics began when the promise of a drink and some supper turned into an excited political gathering as news came through that a major Communist Party official had just resigned. More and more people turned up, and former revolutionaries were suddenly trying to figure out how to fight in an election.

And what they were fighting it for.

The single message the visitors told them over and over was that it was no longer enough to be able to say what they were against. You win elections by telling the electors what you're *for*.

They were never going to learn that from a few days of Civics 101.

And perhaps that's one of the reasons things didn't work out as everyone intended. Perhaps the VPN never quite got to the stage where it had a vision of the future beyond knowing that there wouldn't be any communists in it.

Just because it went wrong in the end, however, doesn't mean that the election was any less worth fighting—or less worth winning.

The sense of pride and purpose lingers. It felt to the Americans then, and it still does today, that what they became involved in was something primal and vital. An episode in history that reminded them all not just of the hard work and drudgery of the democratic process but also of its romance. Its hope. Its importance. Its ability to give people the chance to voice their desires for their own future.

That, at any rate, is how the Americans thought and still do. It's true that some thirty-plus years later, those who had to continue living in Eastern Europe after the revolutions (and whose lives became less involved with politics and more with day-to-day concerns) aren't necessarily still of the same view.

At the time, it was a privilege to see it firsthand.

At a time when politics in the United States is more divisive, coarse, and cheapened than anyone could have imagined only a few years ago, it's important to remember that the democratic system can and does work. It may not be perfect and it may not always give the "right" answer—that being that someone is elected who shares your views on every point—but it's better than the alternative, which is having no voice at all.

There used to be T-shirts one could buy in hippie shops and flea markets with the slogan: "If voting changed anything, they'd abolish it."

It's funny, and it's familiarly cynical about politics. But that doesn't mean it's true. That's not what the people in Slovakia thought. Many had waited for most of their lives to have a chance to vote in a free election.

When that chance came, the young Americans helped them take it. Looking back, it was the purest of times and the purest of elections on which any of them ever worked.

And *damn*, it felt good.

CHAPTER I

GERMINATION

DEMOCRACY IS A GOOD THING.

Any political operative will agree to that. Or at least, most will.

So when democracy started breaking out in Eastern Europe at the end of the 1980s, campaign organizers, strategy wonks, pollsters, voter consultants, and election specialists all over North America—all over the world—watched from the sidelines and cheered. Solidarity was leading change in Poland, the Velvet Revolution had swept Czechoslovakia, and the Berlin Wall had fallen. Country after country was announcing their first free elections in decades. In country after country, the people who had overturned communist rule needed all the help they could get with the nuts and bolts of democracy: forming parties, running campaigns, and attracting voters.

For James Dwinell, publisher of *Campaigns & Elections*, the trade magazine of political consultants in North America, it was a unique opportunity. It was a chance to be involved in a new revolution at the start.

It was as if Thomas Jefferson had called up from Philadelphia and said, "I'm trying to get something off the ground here. Why don't you come down and take a peek? Perhaps you could lend a hand."

Anyone in politics would have taken that call. Dwinell just had to figure out a way to make it pay.

Although *C&E* was a for-profit publication, it actually made more money from running seminars about the practicalities of politics than from selling magazines. For over a decade, Dwinell had been running seminars in the United States and Canada, bringing together expert speakers from various areas of the business. He then expanded overseas into Argentina at the suggestion of a former roommate in the late 1980s. Africa, where he worked for the African-American Institute and the United States Information Agency, was the next place Dwinell took his publication and workshops. The seminars were fun and interesting. They were an opportunity for political advisors to network at a time when the field was getting more professional. They kept the *Campaign & Elections* name prominent in the trade. Above all, they were profitable.

Dwinell knew something about the growing appetite for democracy in Europe. He had traveled in September 1988 to Macedonia, Montenegro, Slovenia, Serbia, and Romania on a month-long journey to talk about that year's US presidential election between George Bush and Michael Dukakis. He had seen how people in the region looked up to the United States and its political system. He had heard people talk about how they admired the way it stood for freedom, democracy, and the American way of life.

Dwinell could see that it was the ideal time to set up

seminars in the former communist states. The problem was figuring out who would pay for them. No one in Eastern Europe had any money.

Two of Dwinell's staff, editor Scott Berkowitz and event and marketing organizer Jennifer Mizrahi, set out to explore possible revenue streams. In particular, they needed to find people who loved democracy and, more to the point, who hated communism so much they thought they could help to destroy it by effectively throwing dollar bills at it.

In 1989, the United States was probably home to more people like that than anywhere else in the world. It was all a little bit like the film *Charlie Wilson's War*.

Berkowitz and Mizrahi approached Spitz Channell, who had been banned from political consultancy work after being found guilty for his role in the Iran Contra scandal. Channel was already busy raising money to overthrow communists via the ballot box as part of a plan to rehabilitate his reputation. Channel showed some interest in the plan, but he got sick with AIDS and died before anything could come to fruition.

Campaigns & Elections tried the National Democratic Institute (NDI), the International Republican Institute (IRI), and the National Endowment for Democracy (NED), all of which, in theory, existed to strengthen democracy around the world. All three said no.

The general view was that while democracy was a good thing—the political consultants' credo—it was possible to have too much of it. The unofficial view from Washington DC was that Soviet leader Mikhail Gorbachev had brought a level of stability to Eastern Europe while dialing down the rhetoric of the Cold War. There was an uneasy calm in the region that the departure of the communists might threaten.

There was also the fact that *Campaigns & Elections* was a

for-profit operation. No nonprofit wanted to be seen to give it money. That was a bad look.

Berkowitz and Mizrahi concluded that the best way to fund the trip was to convince the speakers who would talk at the seminars to pay for the privilege of doing so. Everyone would have to pay their own way to the tune of $5,000 each, which was a huge amount of money at the time. In return, C&E would provide transportation, accommodation, food, and the chance to change the world. The advisers who took part would get a name check in the *Campaigns & Elections* write-up of the trip. If nothing else, it was a chance to network with some of the leading political operatives in North America.

Once Berkowitz and Mizrahi started making calls, it became clear the planned trip had caught the Zeitgeist. People rushed to sign up. Everyone was buzzing about what was happening. The fall of the Berlin Wall, the rise of Lech Walesa in Poland, and the charisma of Václav Havel in Czechoslovakia. Whole populations turned out in city squares that had recently been patrolled by communist guards with machine guns with nothing more than candles and flowers.

Everyone wanted in. Many of those who accepted the invitation were highly credible representatives of a mature democratic system. Others less so. They were idealists, chancers, or drifters who had little idea what precisely they could contribute to the ongoing revolutions, other than by being intrigued enough by politics to have made it their career. That didn't disqualify them, however. The first and most important criterion for getting on the airplane was having a spare $5,000.

The twenty-five people *C&E* eventually recruited were a colorful crew, with Democrats and Republicans, academics and churchmen, human rights experts, and an animal rights activist. They were mainly Americans but with a sizable group of Canadians, and a single representative from South America, the Argentine pollster Felipe Noguera.

FLASHBACK

Andrew Frank was twenty-five years old, and the two stories he saw in early November on the newsstands were: "Florio Wins Big" and "Berlin Wall Falls."

Frank knew about the first story because he had just spent nine months helping Democrat Jim Florio get elected Governor of New Jersey. The second story was more intriguing. Frank knew that Florio's victory had opened the door to a longer political career in New Jersey. Even now, he was busy organizing Florio's inauguration—like a presidential inauguration, with a parade and ball, but smaller, and in New Jersey. There would be other roles afterward, for sure.

But that second headline. "Berlin Wall falls." Frank knew himself well enough to know that he needed to be where the action was. By now, his parents barely reacted when he called home to tell them that he was in a different part of the country, doing something different from what they were expecting. "That's nice, dear, be careful," they would say, with none of the alarm he used to hear in their voices.

Frank's parents had been responsible for his first-ever encounter with a politician, when they took him to the New Jersey Governor's Mansion in 1976. It was open to the public, and Governor Brendan Byrne stuck a small bicentennial red, white, and blue star on Frank's Little League jacket. During high school, he was Freshman class president and participated in other political events, including the anti-nuke rally in Central Park, New York, in 1982. After making his way to Los Angeles for the 1984 Olympics, graduating from college, and sofa-surfing his way across the country, he started volunteering on a few political campaigns. His first "real" campaign was acting as an advance man for Democratic presidential hopeful Michael Dukakis in 1987 and 1988. It proved to be a journey where he learned a ton, met lifelong friends and began to understand the intricacies of local and national politics. The next year he worked for Ron Brown when he became the chairman of the Democratic Party, and after that, he worked for the Florio campaign.

While Frank was mulling over what was going on in Eastern Europe, he happened to talk to one of the friends he'd met on the Dukakis campaign. He told Frank, "Campaigns and Elections Magazine asked me to help set up a tour they're sending to Hungary and Czechoslovakia. I couldn't make the timing work."

Frank said, "Did they find someone else yet?"

"I don't think so. If you're interested, give them a call."

Frank was interested, and he did give C&E a call. James Dwinell told him to come to DC for an interview. Frank leaped at the chance and started learning as much as he could about the situation in Eastern Europe. He needn't have bothered. The interview was largely a formality.

He met with Dwinell, Scott Berkowitz, and Jennifer Mizrahi. They asked him about his experience as an advance man. Frank said, "I turn up in a city a day or two before the candidate to set up venues, accommodation, and press for an event." That was ideal.

They asked him how he felt about being the first boots on the ground in a completely unknown environment. He said, "It's going to be an adventure." Another ideal answer.

They asked him how much he would cost. He asked them how much they had. They told him, "We'll pay you $25 per diem, with your hotels and flights."

It didn't sound very much, but Frank said, "That's fine." This *was yet another ideal answer—and it also turned out to be the correct answer when he found out how comfortably he could live in Eastern Europe on $25 per day.*

For Frank, the trip was a fascinating chance to go overseas and see what was happening close up. It would also be a chance to meet other political consultants and discover more professional opportunities. Frank didn't know what his next career step would be, but he did know that he wasn't ready to settle down back in New Jersey in the governor's office.

For the team at C&E, however, he had another huge advantage.

The final question turned out to be the most important. They asked Frank, "When can you start?"

He said, "Whenever you need me to."

They said, "OK. Well, you need to leave now, because the program is going to be in four weeks." And that was that.

Frank called a flight attendant friend in London. He asked her, "Can I use your apartment as a base for a few weeks? I need somewhere to fly in and out of Eastern Europe."

His friend was quite receptive to the idea (although she would be less so when the plan didn't survive Frank's first contact with practicalities on the ground) so he went ahead and booked a flight to London.

He called his parents to warn them that he didn't know when he'd be back in the States or even able to call them. They were used to it.

"That's nice, dear, be careful."

BEHIND THE CURTAIN

In theory, *Campaigns & Elections* took no sides. It made no sense to alienate any of its particular audience by being politically positioned anywhere other than safely on the fence. Its seminars were neutral events to which the members of any and all political parties were invited. In reality, however, it was soon apparent that the trip couldn't happen without political sponsorship in Eastern Europe, and that would involve dealing with specific parties. The State Department was making it difficult for Americans to get visas for the region, presumably because it feared that too many Charlie Wilsons running around might indeed destabilize the political balance of the region. The unofficial official US view was that Eastern Europe was best left well alone.

C&E reached out to political parties in Budapest, Prague, and Warsaw and began a complex dance around the bureaucracy. It wasn't a question of taking sides; it was simply a question of getting an invitation. Jennifer Mizrahi had to sit by a fax machine and try over and over again to send faxes to long international numbers on unreliable dial-up lines requesting that a party in each country—*any* party—invite the C&E delegates to come. And telling them precisely what the invitation should say, to avoid any doubt. It had to look as if the seminar were the ideas of the respective parties, who had to issue invitation letters.

After many international faxes with half-received messages, illegible documents, and lost signals, Andrew Frank ended up with three letters of invitation, one each in Hungary, Czechoslovakia, and Poland, and the names of three translators. He had little idea how C&E had gotten hold of either.

The idea was that Frank would visit Budapest, Prague, and Warsaw, in turn, identifying venues for the seminars and hotels for the speakers while drumming up interest among local politicians and their advisors. He would repeat the same circuit when the advisors arrived from their respective home countries, getting them settled in one place before jumping ahead to get to the next location set up before they arrived. The $5,000 fee at least entitled the travelers to turn up in a place without having to worry about their own hotels and meals.

Frank's first trip was to Hungary. Stepping off the airplane from London in Budapest, he had no accommodation booked. He simply headed downtown to find somewhere to stay in a city where few people spoke English at the time—though it would turn out they spoke far more than in some of the other cities he would visit. The only hotel he had lined up for the whole trip was a relatively new Holiday Inn in Warsaw, and that was only because, by chance, his father stayed in their sister hotel in Amsterdam, and the GM called ahead.

When it came to making arrangements, Frank was on solid ground. The job requirements were exactly as they were in the States. With his interpreter and fixer, a small man with sandy hair, Frank started doing what he was good at. He went to meet people at the headquarters of different political parties, such as the Hungarian Democratic Forum and the Alliance of Free Democrats and sold them the idea of the *C&E* seminar. As yet, however, he had no idea where it was going to be.

Frank went to the university on the hill overlooking the city, presented himself, and asked to host the seminar there. The university agreed to rent him a large, beautiful room. It was a fairly expensive set-up, with interpreters and translation equipment, not just hard chairs with coffee and danish, and the Hungarians were somewhat reluctant to take someone so young seriously. Frank resembled a young Nikholi Lenin getting off the sealed train in St Petersburg to start the revolution, with his long dark hair and his enveloping trench coat. It was only when the others from C&E turned up, including

Dwinell, that the Hungarians were reassured that they were a real organization with a real publication that held genuine events. And could presumably pay for them.

James Dwinell wanted the first event to be held somewhere impressive in order to set the tone, and Frank had located a spectacular location in a hall belonging to the university on top of the hill on the Pest side of the city, looking over the Danube. It had all the facilities he needed, and that he had tried to replicate at all the venues, with some inevitable variations: one of two large rooms, a handful of smaller break-out rooms, and translation booths and equipment. The university was stately and very, very old. It was hard to ignore the fact that over the centuries, the best brains of Mitteleuropa and the Hapsburg Empire had studied here. They were the people who would go on to invent stuff, run businesses, win Nobel prizes, and rule whole countries.

FLASHBACK

Scott Berkowitz could feel the sweat on his face despite the cool night air. James Dwinell had asked him to take charge of the financial arrangements for the trip, which wouldn't normally have been a problem, because despite his youth (he was nineteen) Berkowitz was academically brilliant, with a sharp, rational mind that meant he could take on virtually any admin task easily. But nothing had prepared him for hurrying along the dark backstreets of Budapest with Andrew Frank and their interpreter—and a gym bag full of wads of bank notes.

Every time he saw a stranger—and to be clear, everyone he saw was a stranger as he'd barely been in town for more than twenty-four hours—he tightened his grip on the bag handles, and his face went clammy.

It didn't help that Andrew Frank, who was technically employed by Scott, seemed to be relaxed about the whole thing. In fact, it was quite clear he rather enjoyed his colleague's discomfiture.

It was all Frank's fault. The dean of the university where Frank had found the rooms he wanted to hire wanted to be paid in Hungarian currency, Forints. And he wanted to be paid in cash.

"What is he, a drug lord?" asked Berkowitz.

"It's just what people do here," Frank reassured him. "And the rooms have lots of space. They're ideal. James will be thrilled."

In truth, the dean was just an academic trying to get reliable funds for his institution. At the time, given how fluid currencies and exchange rates were as Soviet control collapsed, everyone preferred cash over credit or checks—although most people preferred to use US dollars if they could. There was a thriving black market in currency exchange all over Eastern Europe. People were eager to trade their Forints for dollars: the only question was who to deal with. A dollar got you far more Forints on the street than it did at the official Bureau de Change or bank.

Frank explained all this to Berkowitz a few hours earlier. Frank had been in Eastern Europe a couple of weeks longer than the other man, which clearly made him an expert. "The interpreter knows someone who'll give us a better exchange rate. Bring some dollars."

That made Berkowitz nervous. They weren't his dollars, they belonged to C&E. He was already on edge from having to carry enough cash to Europe for the whole fortnight. The currency exchange began when he put what seemed like a lot of that float into an envelope, and waited with Frank for the interpreter.

"What do you know about this guy?"

"Not much. He's some kind of doctor who works with kids. He needs dollars to buy medical equipment from overseas."

The interpreter showed up and led them out of the hotel into the streets of Budapest, where people were going home for the evening. As they passed banks and bureaus de change, Berkowitz wondered whether it might have been easier to simply take the hit and get the money changed officially. At least he might have ended up with a receipt to show James Dwinell what had become of his money.

The three men walked away from the central part of the city. They moved mainly in silence. Berkowitz wondered how Andrew Frank could seem so relaxed.

For his part, Frank was relaxed. While he had only really been doing advance for less than three years, he felt comfortable going off script. It was where he normally operated. In addition, he'd spent almost a month in Eastern Europe now. He felt pretty laid back.

At last, the interpreter stopped outside a large apartment block and rang a bell. The door buzzed open and they stepped into a hallway from where an internal door led into a large courtyard. Berkowitz couldn't relax, although he had to admit to himself that it certainly didn't seem like a den of thieves.

When they got to the right apartment, they were greeted enthusiastically by a short man who smiled while he kept shaking their hands and greeting them in Czech.

"It's a pleasure to meet you," said Frank, and the interpreter passed on the message. The man smiled and nodded as he took them into the kitchen of his small apartment.

"Please," he said in English, gesturing that his guests should sit at a table where he had laid out some bread and a bottle of spirits.

"Thank you," said Frank, sitting and pouring a drink for himself, the translator, and their host. He gestured toward Berkowitz with the bottle. "Are you going to join us?"

No, thought Berkowitz. He wasn't. He didn't feel well. He was only nineteen, barely old enough to drink in a few states in America. The pressure was suffocating. He just wanted to do the deal and get the hell out of there.

"Are you alright?" asked Frank. "You look like you've seen a ghost. Your face has gone a funny shade of gray."

"I'm fine. I just think we should get it over with."

"You should have something. It's only polite. It's what people do here. There's nothing to worry about."

It was clear that Frank really wasn't worried about anything, raising a glass with the interpreter and the doctor who might or might not have been a master criminal.

"Sit," he told his younger colleague. "Have something. We don't want to be rude."

Berkowitz did as he was told, though he couldn't taste the bread and the clear spirit just left a burning sensation in his throat.

Formalities completed, it was time for the transaction to take place. The doctor and translator had already agreed on an exchange rate, which Frank was apparently aware of, though Berkowitz had no way of knowing whether it was favorable or not. He took the envelope out of his jacket pocket and handed it to their doctor friend, who took out the bills inside and started to count them.

The alcohol had made Berkowitz feel light-headed. He heard Frank's voice saying, "Are you ok?" He felt like he was going to pass out. He could barely watch as the doctor completed his count and put the dollars in a neat pile before pulling out a large gym bag. When he opened it, it was full of banknotes. He took out the Forints and started counting, stacking the bills into neat piles as he did so. Berkowitz could feel Frank's anxious eyes on him and could hear him muttering, "Keep your shit together. You look like you're about to piss your pants."

The counting seemed to last forever—there were a lot of Forints. Berkowitz was desperate to say, "I'm sure it's all fine," grab the bag and get out into the fresh air. He was wound up tight and breathing heavily. Eventually, though, the doctor finished counting and confirmed the total with the interpreter, who nodded and said, "It's all there."

Frank turned to Berkowitz and said, "That's it. You're a black-market currency dealer."

Frank was relieved when his colleague's ashen face broke into a small smile. For a while there, he had been seriously worried. He quite enjoyed the adventure of the cloak-and-dagger stuff—it felt like being in a John le Carré thriller—but he could see that the younger man had grown seriously stressed.

The three visitors said their goodbyes and started to walk back to the hotel. Berkowitz clutched the stuffed gym bag tightly. "I don't think this is safe," he told Frank. "It's dangerous carrying this much cash."

"It's fine, Scott. No one knows what's in the bag. There are three of us. No mugger is going to jump three grown men."

Berkowitz was not so sure. Eventually, he saw a taxi and said, "Let's take this cab."

"It's no distance to the hotel."

"I'll feel better if we take a cab. It's much safer."

Frank gave in, and they climbed in the car, Berkowitz clutching the stuffed gym bag on his lap. "You look like someone's trying to take your baby," said Frank.

Frank never asked Berkowitz what he did with the money back at the hotel. Maybe he slept with it that night. It certainly made it intact until the next morning, which was the day of the seminar.

A little while before the event was due to begin, Frank and Berkowitz went to see the Dean. Berkowitz placed the bag of

Forints on his stately wooden desk and opened it, like a crook showing off the protection money he had collected. The Dean smiled as he took the bag. "Thank you. You have your conference. I look forward to it starting this morning."

And that was it. A smooth black market transaction done in the back streets to pay a storied university that was already old when the United States was born with a Dean eager to ensure he made his institution's facilities available for an event that would help shape the future of his country.

Such deals may or may not have been common at the time. It was hard to tell against a background of political flux, with the power and infrastructure of communism failing, parties jostling for position, and the black market thriving. The spirit of excitement and change everywhere was matched by a general feeling of a society on the edge of the law. Crime levels were high, with constant thefts. Gambling, pornography, and prostitution seemed to be everywhere. There were copies of Playboy-style magazines at the checkout of every convenience store.

Frank and the C&E delegation would get used to Europeans asking them "Change, please." What people wanted in all the countries they visited was dollars. But to many of the visitors, the constant request sounded more like a call for a whole new society.

WHAT GOES ON TOUR...

As Frank and Berkowitz finalized arrangements in Budapest, the consultants who had signed up for the C&E trip were on their way from various airports to rendezvous in Frankfurt in Germany before taking the shuttle to Budapest.

Frank had a list of who to expect, with twenty-eight names

and brief biographies. In truth, it wasn't quite as stellar a display of political talent as he had hoped, given that his exposure to top-level talent on the Dukakis presidential campaign had elevated his expectations. But the advisors who arrived had all worked on statewide and federal campaigns. Even if their marquee value was not as high as Susan Estrich, James Carville, or Karl Rove, they had reputations as knowledgeable, successful consultants. In the event, Frank found the people who turned up far more interesting than he had first thought when he saw the list. Some of them were pretty cool to hang out with.

There was Gordy Robson, a businessman, local politician and influence peddler from Canada, with his wife Mary. Gordy bought six places on the tour for various Canadians, so he was quite important to the trip's success. There was Professor David Barber, a political theorist from Duke University who had started writing books about each presidential election campaign, starting in 1968. He gave the trip some academic heft, which delighted Dwinell, as did the general diversity. There were a couple of Republicans, Wayne Johnson from California, and Anne Miller from Texas, who owned a couple of Blockbuster video stores and was eager to let everyone know how close she was to the Bush family. A young activist named Phil Noble—one of the few travelers to have been to the Eastern Bloc before—brought along his father, the Reverend James Noble, who would speak about the church's position in politics in a democracy. Bob White of the International Center for Development Policy in DC was a renegade diplomat who had gotten thrown out of El Salvador by Ronald Reagan. There was an animal rights campaigner and an Argentine pollster.

Trish Whitcomb of Bates Neiman, a specialist in voter contact through direct mail and phone banks, eagerly accepted the invitation to join the trip after her boss passed up the chance. Fascinated since high school by communism as a political philosophy, she embraced her first—and likely last—chance to observe countries still in the shadow of the kind of hard-line communist rule she had heard and read about.

In addition, she lived in Indianapolis, so the cities of Eastern Europe held no fear for her. Nowhere held any fear.

Whitcomb had far more ideas than some of the others as to what they might find on the trip. Her father had been involved in business in the 1980s with János Horváth, a politician and economist who had fled Hungary after the failed revolution of 1956 and now lectured at Whitcomb's alma mater, Butler University. Horváth encouraged her to make the trip and gave her the names of old colleagues to look up. He had been the youngest person elected to the Hungarian parliament right after World War II. After the elections of 1990, he would go back to Hungary, and in 1998 he was elected to parliament again—this time as the oldest member.

From California, Barry Fadem and Kelly Kimball were close friends who had worked together since 1983, traveling up and down California and across the United States getting statewide initiatives on the ballot. Fadem was a campaign lawyer who would write ballot laws. Kimball got them on the ballot, using his petition-management company to gather signatures in shopping malls throughout the state.

For them, the chance to travel to Eastern Europe sounded like fun. The wall having just come down and the Soviet Union having broken up, Kimball could not think of a more exciting place for a young political consultant to be. Having said which, he had absolutely no idea what was going to happen. And even less idea of what he and Fadem could contribute.

The kind of direct democracy they promoted wasn't in the

cards. The countries they were headed to were just finding their way around the whole idea of representative democracy. They had yet to hold their first free candidate elections. It was a little soon to start messing with their heads with talk of referendums and ballot initiatives. No one cared. The fact that they had rustled up $10,000 between them made them as welcome as anyone else on the trip.

Even if they couldn't help, going along was a no-brainer. Kimball looked forward to having drinks and dinner with other US consultants and gathering contacts for the future.

Phil Noble, who was on the trip with his father, had traveled widely when he was younger, touring through Europe and North Africa by minivan and motorbike. He had been to Eastern Europe in 1972 and again in 1976 and had spent a couple of months there. It struck him that they were going on a tour through a parallel political universe from the United States.

Someone on the trip called it the *magical mystery democracy tour*. Most of the C&E people were young enough to be thrilled to liken themselves to Jack Kerouac and his band of crazies touring the States. Their shared love of their craft, their dedication to democracy, and their eagerness to embrace whatever came their way created an electric sense of camaraderie that outweighed any partisanship or national origin.

The audaciousness of what they were doing was wonderful. They were campaign hacks by and large, and they had come to Eastern Europe with the expectation that they had a role to play. And that people would listen to them.

The master of ceremonies was James Dwinell, who was the perfect father figure for the ragtag group. No matter what came up as they headed into the unknown, Dwinell's first reaction was that it wasn't a problem. They would handle it.

Everything would be okay.

Everyone got along well together. Better still, they didn't seem to expect much for their money apart from the chance to actually be there. The traveling by bus was rough, and the hotels and food weren't much better, but no one complained. When someone did, early on, their peers shut them down. Perhaps everyone's expectations were lowered because they didn't know what to expect from Eastern Europe.

Or perhaps they were just too excited to sweat the small stuff.

Although Soviet control of Eastern Europe had been relaxing for a few years, most people in the West were unaware of what life was like behind the Wall. They got their impressions from grainy TV films of drab, imposing apartment blocks where it was almost always raining; comical, boxy little cars; and people standing in line to buy an unappetizing range of food in supermarkets with almost empty shelves. In fact, as Andrew Frank noted on his first trip to Budapest, the Hungarians could buy oranges from Israel, sweaters from the Soviet Union, stereos from America, beer from Germany, and clothes from Italy. And what appeared at first glance to be miniskirts so short they couldn't have come from anywhere else in the world.

There was no Internet at that time to look up where they were going or where they were staying. There was no way they could anticipate what sort of welcome they would receive as representatives of the evil US empire. There were more than a few Eastern Europeans who were still more natural communists than they ever would be free marketeers.

Dwinell's group knew nothing about any of this. They were entering an alien situation where stability was already weak—and they were going to talk about politics. It was hard enough to do at home, where they knew the political scene back to front. When they were walking into a vacuum, it was almost impossible. Which, of course, was one of the things that made it so attractive.

No one knew what was going to happen. Or what the reaction would be.

It was like playing hide and seek as a kid, and you would look around the corner to see if you could find your target— only to find an empty field with beautiful flowers.

The magical mystery democracy tour was about to begin.

CHAPTER 2

BUDAPEST

FLASHBACK

Just hours into their flight to Germany from Los Angeles, Barry Fadem came rushing out of the first-class bathroom and asked Kelly Kimball, "Do you notice anything different about me?"

"Did you put your contacts in?"

"Uh-uh. I dropped my glasses. They went down the toilet."

Seeing his friend's distress, Kimball started laughing—and kept laughing. As Fadem grew more upset, other passengers started laughing too. Soon the whole cabin was laughing hysterically at the American, who already looked as if he had just gotten up, in his sweatpants and T-shirt. When the flight attendants came to help, they started laughing too.

They paused long enough to explain that at Frankfurt they would be able to pass the contents of the toilet through some kind of screen and retrieve the glasses.

That suggestion made Fadem go quiet, as he spent the rest of the flight pondering exactly where his glasses were. And it made Kimball laugh harder still, imagining his friend in a meeting absent-mindedly sucking on the end of glasses recovered from a tank of excrement.

When the plane landed in Frankfurt, the attendants told Fadem they had been kidding. They had fibbed because they wanted him to have a good flight. At which point, the entire cabin erupted into laughter again. And Fadem cried gently because he had been spared a very, very difficult decision.

Glassless, the two men set out through Frankfurt airport to meet their colleagues to start their adventure.

What better way to refresh the jaded air of US politics at the start of the 1990s than an opportunity to help shape the birth of a brand-new democratic system?

Fadem and Kimball assumed that most of their colleagues were experienced international consultants who knew exactly what they were going to say about candidate elections. In fact, few of the group that boarded the shuttle to Budapest had any idea what they would find or how they would be received.

The Iron Curtain had divided Europe for longer than many of them had been alive. It loomed so large in the Western imagination that heading behind it came with an extra edge of hilarity—and fear. What was more, they were going to be talking to people who were far more serious than they were about politics. For whom it wasn't a career or a logistical challenge, or even an intriguing intellectual pastime. They were going to meet people who had spent long periods of their time imprisoned not because of their political views but simply because they thought they should have the right to have political views.

The Gypsy party in Hungary had a button showing a person kneeling on the ground with their hands tied behind their back. You were only entitled to wear the button if you'd been locked up as a political prisoner. And when the gypsies came to the seminar, they were all wearing it.

On the other hand, as Andrew Frank had discovered on his initial trip, their hosts in Eastern Europe didn't dismiss the interest from outside. They embraced it.

The idea that experts from North America would come and teach the elements of democracy for free was strangely reassuring to political activists who had spent most of their lives in a thankless fight against Big Brother. If nothing else, it was a sign that others believed in them, and that helped them believe in themselves. It made them feel they were being admitted to the club they had long admired.

In most countries, a few perceptive observers were beginning to appreciate that getting rid of communism might have been the easy part. Setting up a democracy suddenly seemed a far greater challenge.

The idea that a group of foreigners would fly to their country and speak to them in an organized, serious way in fine state rooms fitted with headsets and with interpreters in their own booths, rather than in hidden cellars or furnace rooms, made democracy very real. At the time, there was still a huge amount of fear of the consequences of joining in the democratic revolution, and many people were hesitant to take part. Around a fifth of the population were still somehow connected to the Communist Party, so the idea of supporting another party was really frightening. And the idea of giving information to political campaigners, signing up for anything, even answering the door to canvassers, or getting in the back of a van for a ride to the polling station were more frightening still.

HOME FROM HOME

Trish Whitcomb had been fascinated since high school with the idea of what life was like behind the Iron Curtain. When she finally got there, the experience was more surreal than she could have imagined.

Her hotel was a Marriott. Most signs were in English. But most of all, the first thing she saw when she switched on the TV in her room was a video fellow Hoosier John Mellencamp had produced for Bob Dylan, "Living in the Political Word." Kids she had grown up with in small-town Seymour, Indiana, were performing on a small screen in her hotel room in Budapest. What the heck!

Before she left, she had asked Mellencamp for some free cassettes to give out to doormen or whoever else she met. With commendable foresight, he had reckoned that country rock would be most popular behind the Iron Curtain. Always a keen marketer, he sent along tapes of some of the lesser-known artists on his label, eager to get some publicity.

Whitcomb had also taken twenty energy bars with her in case she wasn't able to eat the local food. It was a sensible precaution—and a very Hoosier thing to do. The food and drink in the countries they visited were cheap, but it was of variable quality, inevitably heavy with meat and sausages and swimming in sauce. It was strangely reassuring to be able to pull open the sealed foil wrapper of a bar she knew well.

The group stayed in a hotel by the Chain Bridge, looking over the river to the Pest side. Andrew Frank supplied maps of the city for everyone in case they wanted to go exploring, and there were optional tours if anyone wanted to take them. People visited the Great Market Hall, which was full of food vendors and looked like the kind of place where James Bond might come running through at any time, chased by the villains. Others were happier with McDonald's, evidence, much like the prominent Adidas Shop, that Hungary was moving into the modern world pretty quickly.

Trish Whitcomb found her way to a trolley stop and went to look at other parts of the town. The buildings changed as she traveled out from the central city. Beyond the historic center, the buildings were shabbier, the people poorer, and the atmosphere more deadening.

Barry Fadem meanwhile helped himself get over the trauma of losing his glasses on the airplane by finding a casino. Again, it was straight out of a James Bond movie.

No Hungarians were allowed inside. Not even as workers.

The blackjack dealers were all German or Austrian, and the guests were a mixture of central Europeans and North Americans. They didn't even use Hungarian money; only British Pounds Sterling, German Deutsche Marks, and US Dollars. Even in Budapest, a casino wasn't going to load the odds against the house by dealing in Forints.

Fadem had a good night at the casino. When he came to cash in his stack of chips, Kelly Kimball asked how much he had won, and Fadem told him, "Ten or twelve bucks, or something like that." Fadem went to the cashier's window and passed over his winnings. It was only when the cashier started counting off dollar bills that he realized he had been playing in German Deutsche Marks and that his estimation of his winnings had been somewhat conservative.

Fadem walked out with over a thousand dollars. Which was nothing like as much as he'd left on the table. "For the Hungarian economy," he said.

GETTING STARTED

Andrew Frank and Scott Berkowitz's gym bag of Forints had bought rooms for the seminar at the Karl Marx University, which had been renamed the Budapest University of Economics earlier in 1990 as part of the dismantling of the communist state. The idea was that everyone in the C&E party would speak or run workshops twice during the course of the two days.

It didn't start well.

The Canadian Gordy Robson, who had paid to bring five associates on the trip, claimed that his role in underwriting the whole operation gave him the right to welcome the delegates to the event. James Dwinell was equally determined that he would do it, as the publisher of the magazine that had organized the whole trip. It was not an auspicious start, particularly when the pair had something of a shouting match, fueled in part by adrenaline and in part by the wired tiredness of jetlag.

When the bust-up was through, Dwinell kicked off the seminar. The audience was smaller than he and Frank had hoped. By the time the *Campaigns & Elections* team got to Budapest, the elections were only a couple of weeks away. It was no time for anyone to sign up for their first Politics 101. In addition, Dwinell had resisted attempts by the Hungarian authorities to take control of the event. The Hungarians had told him, "If you don't do this through us, there won't be anyone at your event," but he had ignored the threats.

Now many of the key players stayed away. Perhaps they would have done so, anyway, with the elections being so close. Not that anyone really knew who the key players were, anyway.

Andrew Frank was getting ready to head to the next stop, Bratislava in Slovakia, but he was concerned about the lack of enthusiasm. He reasoned that the political parties couldn't spare many people to waste their time sitting in a room with Americans telling them what they had to do when they thought they already knew. The Hungarians had been agitating for elections since before the fall of the Berlin Wall in November 1989. The dismantling of the communist state was more advanced there than in much of Eastern Europe, and the parties had been preparing for almost eighteen months. So while they were interested in how to win votes, they didn't have much time to listen to the visitors.

Frank had already observed on his first visit that the Hungarians were a little different from the other East Europeans. A little arrogant. A little more superior in their tone, as befitted their imperial past and their close historical links with Austria and Germany. In the other cities on the tour, people greeted him by asking, "Oh, can you help us?" and "Can we buy you a drink?" In Budapest, the Hungarians who Frank met tended to ask the sort of questions you might ask a gatecrasher at a wedding, questions like "Who are you?" and "Why are you here?"

MINORITY ISSUES

A few C&E people were a little unhappy with the low-key debut, but most barely noticed. The rooms were huge and beautiful, and the city was fascinating; all in all, it was a great dry run for the rest of the tour. Most of all, it was simply so exciting. They were a bunch of wide-eyed kids, with jet lag, peeking into a totalitarian world that had been closed for almost the whole of their lives.

What was there to complain about?

Frank had been in touch with ten or fifteen of Hungary's

political parties—they were legion—including the Democratic Forum and Fidesz, the Alliance of Free Democrats, and the Socialist Party, which was made up of members of the former communist government. He'd reached out to the Independent Smallholders Party, which was a more agrarian party, and the Social Democratic Party of Hungarian Gypsies. The visitors were infatuated by the beautiful women with huge hoop earrings who arrived with their male colleagues in a big truck. They stood out for their different clothes, their different way of doing things, and their distinctive pins.

The Gypsies' presence immediately raised issues about minority rights. None of the advisors could ignore the open hostility of many of the people in the room—and outside in the city—towards Gypsies, Jews, and nearly everyone else who was perceived as belonging to a minority. For forty-five years, the communists had controlled such prejudice by simply outlawing it, but now everyone spoke openly of their dislike of Gypsies, Jews, and Slovaks.

It was shocking. One of Phil Noble's talks at the seminar was about minority rights in a majority government. His audience got excited about the question of what happened if just one, two, or three people objected to something. The Hungarians wanted to know if you needed to make allowances for a handful of objectors, and take their views into account, or if you could just govern by absolute majority. Noble told them that the system always gives the minority some rights. Someone else raised their hand and asked, "Well, what do you do at the end if they never agree to anything?" A heated debate broke out among the Hungarians as they went back and forth. Then a dour old guy at the front of the room, who Noble had pegged as a former communist, raised his hand and said, "This is very simple. All you have to do is shoot them."

It was clear the Hungarians were approaching the election from a totally different starting place with completely different rules of engagement. It struck Noble at the time that it could take them at least a generation to get together the sort of functioning democracy that the rest of the world would recognize. They were less interested in looking to the future than in returning to the past, skipping back over the whole communist period to return to a pre-communist world they saw as a golden age of purely Hungarian culture in which antisemitism and nationalism had never stopped being corrosive issues.

To counter that bleak outlook, Noble found a reason for optimism in the Fidesz party. They were a young, entrepreneurial group of economic liberals whose symbol was an orange. They wanted to get rid of a lot of old social institutions. One of them told him politics was no place for anyone over thirty-five years old.

A couple of years later, Fidesz pivoted hard to the right. They remain in power in Hungary, still led by one of the original young idealists who had impressed Noble, Viktor Orbán. Today, Orbán has a reputation as one of Europe's most vocal authoritarians, and his scorn of outsiders and minorities reflects some of the worst prejudices the C&E advisors heard in Budapest decades ago.

By the morning of the seminar, when Frank and Berkowitz were placing their bag of Forints on the Dean's desk in the university, it was too late to teach the Hungarians anything about how to run a campaign. That late in the day, it was just a question for the individual parties of how they might be able to convince a few more people to vote for them on election day. Most of the fifteen parties were little more than a few people with little idea about reaching out to prospective voters.

The activists proudly showed off their campaign literature. One of them had a sheet of mimeographed paper with a list of the 200 reasons that you should vote for whatever political party they represented, all in such a small font that no one would ever read it for any reason unless they were forced to do so as some kind of punishment.

It broke virtually every rule of campaign literature in the United States.

More striking was a large poster that came to symbolize the trip. It showed the back of a thick-necked departing Soviet soldier with the slogan "Goodbye Comrades."

When *Time* magazine did a brief article on the trip—press attention was generally hard to come by—that was the poster they used to illustrate the piece.

It struck Reverend James Noble, who gave a workshop with David Barber on the relationship between church and state, that the Hungarians were not interested in imitating Western politics. They admired the United States, but they were wary of the ills of capitalism. They wanted to have a system that would work for them. Barber told them, "You are the Washingtons and Jeffersons of Hungary. You are at the place in which Washington, Jefferson, and Madison established our government by having to work out a lot of details about democracy. You arrive in that place in your country. And it's important that you develop a kind of democracy that will work for you."

CHUCKLE BROTHERS

Kelly Kimball and Barry Fadem had been trying to figure out the best contribution they could make to the seminars. Since every other consultant on the trip would be talking about candidate elections, Kimball and Fadem faced the challenge of talking about an initiative process—getting new laws on the ballot—that was completely unknown behind the Iron Curtain. In the end, they improvised a kind of routine about the future shape of democracy in Eastern Europe in which Kimball played the role of a voter who was in favor of direct democracy initiatives, and Fadem played the role of a legislator who was hell-bent on defending representative democracy and the legislative process. One of Fadem's roles was to decry the stupidity of voters in general, for example, while arguing that this meant that only smart people could or should be the legislators who would make all the decisions for the country. The response of Kimball's voter was to point out that, since the legislative system made it impossible to get rid of bad politicians, it was absolutely necessary for the voters to have the right to put legislative proposals on the ballot.

Fadem enjoyed the routine because he got to call his partner a dumb, ignorant asshole every night on stage. Kimball enjoyed it because it meant that Fadem did at least half the talking.

It was straight out of *Saturday Night Live*. Comedy gold.

It soon became less laughable in the face of naked antisemitism and prejudice. It became clear that if the Hungarians were to implement something like an initiative process, the majority could easily go ahead and vote to exterminate all Jews or destroy minority communities. So Kimball and Fadem began to stress how important it was to establish a strong constitution that protects minorities before direct democracy was even possible. For the rest of the trip, the pitch changed to a simple message: "You don't want to use the initiative process right now. Not until you get a strong constitution. Forget it."

Kimball and Fadem probably spoke to a room of twenty

people, not one of whom understood what they were saying. Kelly misunderstood James Dwinell's signal as he brought his hands together in front of him and then pulled them apart at shoulder height. Dwinell's sign was intended to tell Kimball to slow down, to stretch things out, but he just kept going at the same speed. Dwinell got more and more frustrated, knowing the speed at which the two were speaking was too fast for the interpreters to translate without taking shortcuts, which made their messages less intelligible.

Hungarian is a complex and full language. Interpreters need 40 percent more time to express English words in Hungarian words, so speakers have to slow down their conversation.

As Dwinell kept gesturing, Kimball made the opposite mistake. He started to speed up. The interpreter didn't stand a chance. Nor did the delegates, who ended the session as unfamiliar with the ideas of referendums and ballot initiatives as they were when they began.

GETTING ALONG

Meanwhile, the people on the C&E tour were getting to know one another. About the only thing they had in common was that they knew nothing and had no international experience. They were innocents abroad. Babes in the woods. They probably wouldn't have ended up carrying a duffle bag full of money if there had been anyone from the State Department involved. Or if one of the big beasts from the world of political consultancy had turned up. Then all the newbies would have genuflected.

The lack of a dominant personality—even the charismatic Canadian, Gordy Robson—fostered a feeling that they were all in it together. After all, they were surrounded by former Commies, so they needed to stick together. This had been enemy territory just a few months earlier.

No one who had watched *Red Dawn* in their formative years could forget that.

It was just as well that they all got on, as they all shared the same bubble for a couple of weeks. Kelly Kimball feared it was a recipe for discord. He didn't see how he was going to hit it off with Republicans, of which there were a couple. Wayne Johnson wasn't only a Republican, for goodness sake. He was a conservative, evangelical Republican with views antithetical to Kimball's own.

So Kimball was surprised to realize that they got along because their personalities were more similar than they were different. They might have different views, but their interest in politics as a process was stronger than their differences over policy. They shared the same outlook.

As an initiative consultant, Kimball rarely got to interact on any kind of political party level. He never got to meet the "enemy"—although at least he believed he knew who the enemy was. As a committed liberal (he described himself as "left of Mao") his enemies were those Republicans on the evangelical right—like his new traveling companion, Wayne Johnson.

He couldn't have been more wrong. Not only was Johnson great company. His down-to-earth attitude to life was one of the highlights of Kimball's time in Europe. It awoke a realization that not all Republicans were bad by any means that had a profound influence on how Kimball treated those with different political views from his own going forward. Although he knew Mao would probably not have approved.

Budapest was the warm-up act for the rest of the tour. In

many ways, it was something of a disappointment, with the low attendance, the hostile views, and the difficulties with translation. But the audience was engaged and asked interesting questions.

In other words, questions other than simply, "Why are you here?"

At the end of the seminar, people started coming up to James Dwinell to thank him for being there. They said that the seminar was an important step in their development and they were grateful for the faith he showed in them. The United States was the beacon that had modeled democracy to them for decades, and now people from the United States were among those describing what they could do.

Three decades later, after the assault on the Capitol and the Big Lie of the 2020 presidential election, that would come to seem highly ironic.

CHAPTER 3

BRATISLAVA

FLASHBACK

"Politics surely makes strange bedfellows," thought Trish Whit-comb as she looked out of the window of the Mercedes driving her from Budapest to Bratislava. The same could be said for luxury travel. Whitcomb had caught wind of the fact that Felipe Noguera, the pollster from Argentina, and Ann Miller, the Republican fundraiser from Texas, had decided to hire a driver with a Mercedes to take them the 125 miles from Budapest to Bratislava rather than going on the bus. It didn't take her long to figure out that the $100 investment would be money well spent.

For one thing, the driver spoke passable English, which she hoped would allow her and her colleagues to explore some charming villages along the way. For another thing, the seats would be much more comfortable.

Unlike some of her other colleagues on the trip, Whitcomb had no problem with Republicans. In fact, she and Ann Miller shared a common thread that ran through the Bush family. Whitcomb's father had informally assisted on George H.W. Bush's campaign in 1988 because Dan Quayle was on the ticket, and Quayle had worked in Edgar Whitcomb's office when he was governor of Indiana. Whitcomb had been brought up able to cheerfully wine and dine with the most conservative Republican without heartburn.

As it was, Whitcomb and Miller were in any case united by their curiosity about Noguera, whose homeland was in a period of political turmoil. Mercifully, his English was much better than their Spanish and he was happy to answer their questions: about the inflation crisis, "the disappeared," and life that cycled between dictators and military control. His responses were intelligent but full of emotion, and Miller and Whitcomb tacitly refrained from giving their personal opinions about the role played by American foreign policy in Argentina's turbulence.

For Whitcomb, that wasn't that she didn't have opinions. She had many. But the whole point of choosing to travel in the Mercedes was to enjoy some relaxed camaraderie, not to stoke political discord.

The three chatted amiably as the Hungarian countryside slipped by. Then the driver started to slow and told them they were approaching the Czechoslovakian border. Whitcomb didn't think much more about it. It was common knowledge among the C&E crowd that not every citizen of the countries they were visiting was ecstatic about the end of communist rule, but she assumed that crossing the border would be relatively painless. After all, they were there at the invitation of official political parties in each separate country.

It turned out that didn't please the Czech border guards. Well, something didn't please them.

They were large, burly men with stern faces that were frozen into scowls. And they started hitting the car, pounding on the hood with their fists and then banging on the sides of the car as they surrounded the occupants. Who were, frankly, terrified.

"What on earth?" thought Whitcomb. It struck her that perhaps the men took exception to the notion that traveling should be relaxing or comfortable. Or was it the German car? Or was it the fact that the foreigners' visas showed that they had been invited to Czechoslovakia by VPN, Public Against Violence, which was the party working hardest to move Czechoslovakia away from communism?

Whatever the cause, one thing was certain. These guys were pissed. And, it seemed to Whitcomb, they were exactly the kind of low-level functionaries who would be reluctant to say goodbye to the government that had given them their status and some material advantages.

As the guards kept banging on the side of the car, Whitcomb, Miller, and Noguera looked at each other inside. Whitcomb could see the concern on her companions' faces. Whatever was happening, Whitcomb thought, it didn't seem like a situation that could be diffused by handing over a couple of John Mellencamp's country-rock cassettes.

The guards made the three passengers get out of the car and take their luggage from the trunk. They made the travelers open their suitcases, which they proceeded to search.

Whitcomb's first thought was, "I hope they don't take my snack bars." Honestly, she didn't think she could get through the trip without them. But even that concern wasn't enough to stop her cringing as she watched the guards rifling through her underwear.

There was nothing in the suitcases. Of course. So then the guards performed a methodical search on the whole car. Whitcomb and the others watched, getting impatient but also vaguely concerned. Whitcomb thought, "What are they looking for?"

When they found nothing, the guards simply said, "Okay. Bye."

To Whitcomb, it was an anticlimax. "Okay. Bye." As they drove away into Czechoslovakia, she felt cross and frustrated. The guards had given no word of explanation. There was no word of explanation of what they were looking for or why they had picked on the Mercedes. In Whitcomb's imagination, the men might have been nervous about terrorism, although she quickly reasoned that pounding on the hood would not have been a smart way to check whether a car was carrying a bomb.

"They did it because they could," said Ann Miller, and Noguera agreed. So, on reflection, did Whitcomb. The guards had put them through the wringer simply to intimidate them. Because even as communist power faded around them, they still could.

Maybe that was the frustration they were taking out on the foreigners. Or maybe they were just like petty officials everywhere.

Petty.

That encounter with the former communist bureaucracy shook Whitcomb, but it still didn't prepare her for the revelation that was to come when the travelers reached the city limits of Bratislava. Whitcomb had grown up with a romantic view of planned economies, and the seemingly egalitarian lifestyle communism could afford its people, which she suspected was far more successful and just than her teachers and her father insisted. It was a romantic vision shared by many young political activists in the United States—and it barely lasted a moment after coming into contact with reality.

In the twilight, Whitcomb could see in the distance an apartment complex that made Cabrini Green in Chicago look like midtown Manhattan duplexes. *The towering buildings were like concrete boxes, precariously stacked one upon another. It was nothing like the kind of workers' paradise she had sometimes imagined. Later Whitcomb learned that 100,000 people had been relocated by the communists from other locations in Czechoslovakia to work in an aluminum plant on the Danube in Bratislava.*

It was a moment of great consequence for Whitcomb—and a day of rapid growing up. As she stared at the grim buildings in the distance, she began to understand for the first time the difference between reading about political philosophy in the comfort of her classroom in Seymour and seeing firsthand what communism meant to everyday people.

Whitcomb's sobering realization had been echoed by the experience of the members of the group who had arrived in Bratislava by bus. They were not feeling particularly welcome. Barry Fadem and Kelly Kimball came down to the hotel lobby once to find three or four die-hard communists harassing other members of the C&E group. The police had to come to remove them so that the visitors could come and go without being intimidated. For the first time, the atmosphere on the trip echoed the fault lines of the Cold War, with the open wariness of—and hostility toward—the representatives of the free-market economy.

THIS ISN'T KANSAS

They arrived in Bratislava under cover of darkness.

This was why, the next morning, they woke up, looked out the window, and thought, "Oh my God." The sky was gray and gloomy, and so were the buildings. The mood was gray and gloomy. There was an old town with cobbled streets and the VPN headquarters in the Mozart House. Andrew Frank had noted on his first visit that the city was divided between its beautiful old town, with the castle on the hill, and the dull, Soviet-style apartment buildings across the river.

They weren't in Kansas anymore. Or even in the Marriott in Budapest. Compared to Bratislava, Budapest was a fairy-tale palace straight out of Disneyland. Apart from its small center, Bratislava was gloomy, gray skies; gloomy, gray buildings; and gloomy, gray people. The shops were old and beaten down. The buildings were squat and ugly. The factories were the factories of industrial nightmares.

The Reverend James Noble's camera was stolen while he and his son, Phil, were checking into the hotel. This theft followed two incidents in Hungary where Phil's bag and passport and Kelly Kimball's camera had been stolen. Petty crime seemed to be rife. Perhaps, Andrew Frank thought, Scott Berkowitz had been right to push him to take a cab with the gym bag full of cash in Budapest. The Nobles reported the camera theft to the concierge. Three hours later, the desk called up and gave them directions to a police station. They went down a deep, winding alley and found the police station. When they went inside, there was the camera sitting on a desk, ready to be handed back.

People told them that there had been a 100 percent increase in crime since the fall of communism. But enough of the communist security apparatus remained in place to make solving crimes pretty straightforward.

OVERLOOKED REVOLUTION

When the party from *Campaigns & Elections* headed for Eastern Europe, most of them would have been hard-pushed to find Bratislava on a map. A few hadn't even heard of it.

Yet for a handful of the advisors, the side trip to the industrial town, then the regional capital of Slovakia—soon to become the national capital—would become the most important part of the whole trip. It drew them out of the neutrality that underlay the C&E trip and compelled them to take sides among the parties jostling for political support. It would bring them together with revolutionaries who were building democracy from the ground up. It would give them a chance to affect real lives in a way people like them rarely, if ever, experienced in the United States. It would derail the itinerary for the tour and change lives not just for the coming days but forever.

And, entirely unwittingly, it would become a tiny cog in the gigantic grinding of gears that ultimately helped break Czechoslovakia in two by allowing the Slovaks to prepare the democratic framework that would eventually support their ultimate break with the Czech Republic. Which was remarkable given that this part of the trip was an afterthought.

Bratislava hadn't been on the original itinerary for the trip, which was Budapest, Prague, and Warsaw. When Andrew Frank was doing advance reconnaissance in Prague, however, he met people from Civic Forum, the party that had led the Velvet Revolution against communism and now made up the temporary Czechoslovakian government under President Václav Havel. Someone from Civic Forum mentioned that the party had a Slovakian sister movement, Public Against Violence (VPN), based in Bratislava. The parties stood on much the same platforms but were independent, each intending to put up its own slate of candidates in its own region when federal elections eventually happened.

Perhaps, the Czechs suggested to Frank, VPN might be interested in what the visitors had to say.

Frank checked with *C&E* in Washington DC. The length of the tour was fixed, so time for Bratislava would have to be carved out of the three other venues, but Dwinell, Berkowitz, and Mizrahi thought it sounded interesting. The group would need some type of official invitation to enable them to get visas. But if Frank could sort out that information and guarantee that there'd be enough interest to make it worthwhile, he could go ahead and make the arrangements.

On Frank's trip to Bratislava, it turned out that the VPN *were* interested in what the visitors had to say. So interested, in fact, that they volunteered their headquarters as a venue for the seminar: the beautiful Mozart House in the equally beautiful Old Town, once a capital of the Hapsburg Empire, which seemed almost out of place surrounded by the gloom of the communist city.

Budapest had been full of Westerners; Prague was, too. Business people, tourists, and political advisors were arriving from Western Europe and the States. The National Endowment for Democracy was sending advisors and observers. Volunteers and professionals all wanted in on the action.

There was no one in Bratislava, apart from an occasional fleeting visitor.

The city was in the south of Czechoslovakia, traditionally more industrial than the north. And poorer. And less well-educated. James Dwinell had heard that it had the lowest level of college participation in all of Europe except for Albania. Many Slovaks felt that Prague was not taking care of its roads, its bridges, or its education. They resented it. More and more were beginning to argue that you could be a Czech politician or a Slovak politician—but not both. (A quick history lesson: Czechoslovakia had been formed only in 1918, after World War I, from four previously unconnected provinces, including

Slovakia. The people spoke in different dialects and, in some parts, an entirely different language).

That was a fault line that would have immense consequences in the future.

This was why the *Campaigns & Elections* gang who eventually arrived from their first event in Budapest found such willing listeners.

If you were about to fight your party's first federal election—in fact, your *country's* first federal election—the visitors might not have been the team you would have picked if you had much choice. They themselves would admit they were not necessarily the A Team compared to some of the better-known experts and consultants who had turned up in Budapest and Prague. The cream of the US political machine had shipped en masse to take part in the process of delivering democracy to the Eastern Bloc.

But in Bratislava, the visitors were the A-Team. Apart from some businessmen, who were mainly from neighboring Austria, and some Germans helping the Christian Democrats, the *Campaigns & Elections* advisors were the only people paying attention to VPN and its cause.

That's how Andrew Frank ended up meeting Andrei Bartosevicz, who was head of VPN's department of foreign relations, and Juraj Mihalik, a member of the Coordinating Committee of the Revolution who was going to run the election campaign.

In fact, Andrei and Juraj spoke the best English among the senior members of the VPN, so they met all foreign visitors.

While they were talking about the seminar, Juraj suggested that Frank should arrange for some of the visitors to have dinner at his home, a large apartment in the center of town, on the evening of the seminar. Frank accepted the invitation on their behalf—though by then, he himself would be in Prague, preparing the next stage of the tour.

GUESS WHO'S COMING TO DINNER

Before Frank moved on, he was around long enough to see that the seminar in Bratislava was packed, much to his relief after the disappointment of Budapest. About 150 people came along. Frank didn't really care who showed up, just so long as there were people in the seats. The Christian Democrats came, with a few other stragglers, but most of the delegates were associated with Public Against Violence. VPN was less a political party than a movement. It had originally been formed as an umbrella for the many parties preparing for the first democratic elections, all of whom were supposed to be welcome at the Mozart House—but as the building became the VPN campaign headquarters, it became a less neutral location.

The day of talks at the Mozart House went well. VPN participants were highly engaged, with a lot of interaction, and the advisors had learned how to work with interpreters more effectively than in Budapest. At least, Kelly Kimball had learned to slow down enough to give the interpreter a chance to breathe, let alone to speak. This was more like it. With elections happening three months later in June, the timing was perfect. This time they felt that they might actually have a contribution to make other than keeping casinos in business.

The invitation to dinner with some of the VPN activists didn't seem to have any particular political significance. Frank had arranged other similar chances for small groups to meet with European activists during the trip. However, the visitors who went—Kelly Kimball, Barry Fadem, Trish Whitcomb, Greg Lyle, and Ginny Kotnick—felt honored to be invited into someone's home, especially after the seminar, when it was clear that VPN were extremely attentive to what they had to say. At the very least, they'd be able to increase the chemistry they were already developing among themselves, and there was always the hope of some good food and free alcohol. Their host, a ceramicist named Juraj Mihalik, was notable not only for having traveled in the West—hence his ability to speak English—but also for the fact that the communist government allowed him to make and sell his ceramics as a private venture in a communist state.

In one word, Juraj was an entrepreneur. In Eastern Europe in the late 1980s, that was a singular CV, and there was something mysterious about him. He seemed much more worldly than his colleagues, with his languages and his globe-trotting. On his very first meeting, Frank had noted in his diary that Juraj was "an outstanding guy." Mihalik told his guests that, as a young man, he had opted not to go to the military but instead to pursue a career in art. Not only did the state allow this, but it commissioned him to make public art before he started selling ceramic objects in a stall at the farmer's market. The state paid him upfront and also a royalty to make ceramics that people could use in their homes.

It was the sort of story that would have had John le Carré's imagination running wild.

But if Juraj's background and his relationship with the state were mysterious, there was no doubting his sincere desire for change.

Juraj, who seemed to know everyone in Bratislava, might have been VPN's de facto ambassador, but he wasn't a political strategist or an ideas guy. The real political figures were Fedor Gál and Ján Budaj. Fedor Gál, a co-founder of VPN, was a social scientist and researcher who had been born inside

Terezin concentration camp. Ján Budaj was one of the main people who stood up and talked at VPN meetings and rallies.

It was quiet when the visitors arrived, but more people kept drifting in. Soon, Juraj's apartment resembled a student party, with people sitting around on cushions drinking Bull's Blood red wine from half-gallon bottles. It was the sort of gathering where people come up with a plan to eradicate global poverty that they know for sure will work but can't remember the next day. The kind of talking shop most people grow out of soon after leaving university.

This time, it turned out to be one of the most formative evenings of their lives. And, as it turned out, of Slovakian history.

As the evening went on, more people turned up until there were twenty or more. The visitors didn't recognize the bearded men or the graceful women who filled the room, but they were earnest and eager to question their guests about the political process. Many were not much older than the North Americans, wearing corduroy jackets and high-waisted trousers. They looked like a Country & Western band at a bar in small-town Texas. In fact, they included most of the leaders of VPN.

The Slovaks were a mixture of writers, artists and academics, lawyers and laborers who had in common only the fact that between them, they had managed to overthrow the communist government. Many were almost as young as their visitors, although others were in their middle age. One gentleman in his sixties, Milan Šimečka—he was accompanied by his son Martin—was a leading Czech dissident and philosopher who had been imprisoned for his role in writing Charter 77.

That document, secretly written in 1976, boldly demanded that the communist government respect international human rights agreements signed since the end of World War II. Many of the 300 dissidents who had signed the charter in 1976 became negotiators with the communists during the Velvet Revolution in the late 1980s. Nothing about Milan Šimečka's quiet demeanor and modest mannerisms suggested the heroic role he had played with his colleagues of standing toe-to-toe with the communists in the fight for democracy.

VPN had originally come together as conspirators, but now they gathered as members of the interim government that had taken over Slovakia after the Velvet Revolution. It was clear to the visitors that such gatherings had been common during the years of suppression. In their heads, many of those crowded into the apartment remained activists who enjoyed mildly drunken debates about philosophy, beliefs, and principles.

At one stage in the evening, Juraj received a phone call. He spoke briefly before running to turn on the TV, calling for everyone's attention. On screen, the prime minister of Slovakia was publicly renouncing her membership in the Communist Party.

It was a remarkable symbol of the spirit of change filling the room.

Juraj broke out more bottles of Bull's Blood as the momentous event sank in, and his colleagues started going around in a circle telling their stories of when, how, and why they had started going to the city's main square, where protests against the communist government had been going on for months. Every time people had gone to the square, they had been crushed. Many had been arrested or jailed. Some had been barred from their jobs in punishment. College professors were forced to take jobs such as shoveling coal into furnaces in apartment buildings just to earn a living.

In fact, some of them actually quite enjoyed the work

because it gave them plenty of time to read. It turns out you don't have to shovel coal into a furnace very often.

One story was particularly vivid for Trish Whitcomb. A man told her how he was arrested for owning a book, De Tocqueville's *On Democracy in America*. The authorities came and ransacked the office he had as part of his government job. They found his contraband book, and he lost his job.

The Slovaks told stories of people being arrested or shot, even killed, but everyone in the room had all made an individual decision at some point to go down to the square, even though they fully understood they might die there. Some of them had met in prison. But the planning and organizing that eventually propelled the idea of democracy in Bratislava continued. The activists who took part called it "the Public Secret."

Then came the day when 200,000 people turned up in the square, and the communist government collapsed. The institutions at the heart of the state crumbled. Suddenly, the leaders of the protests were the new government. In all the uncertainty and turmoil, their fellow Slovaks looked to them and expected them to know what to do.

And they weren't ready.

They knew they were against communism—but they didn't really know how to turn that into being *for* something. They knew they wanted to give people more chances to realize their self-worth through economic change and privatization, for example, but they disagreed about how much and about how it could be achieved.

It was not a unique problem. After the Berlin Wall fell and then the Iron Curtain, people in different countries in Eastern Europe faced the same challenge. There were some parallels later with what happened in the Middle East after the Arab Spring started in 2010.

Former rebels aren't always the best people to learn how to govern. In fact, they've often proved some of the very *worst* people to govern.

The people the Americans were talking to were figuring out how to create a political party and a government from scratch. How could the guests not be excited? They drank wine and listened to stories of the revolution—told by the revolutionaries themselves—with a growing conviction that they could help.

To begin with, the conversation was limited by the fact that only a handful of the Slovaks spoke English, who translated for the rest, some of whom even took notes. Later on, for the last few hours, everyone finally went home at about 4:00 a.m. It was limited because everyone had had too much Bulls' Blood.

Or were, in any case, drunk on the spirit of the revolution.

For a few hours in the middle of the evening and into the small hours, however, the place was on fire as dialogue moved back and forth.

VPN leaders were eager to gain any tips they could about the approaching elections that their opponents hadn't gained during the official seminar. In particular, they were concerned about the Christian Democrats. The Christian Democrats had the advantage of advice from sister parties in Austria and Germany. They were led by an experienced lawyer, Ján Čarnogurksý, who had been vice-prime minister in the interim government led by Václav Havel.

Compared to them, VPN was a herd of cats. They were worried they would get their asses kicked. "We started this fire. We started the revolution that broke the government, and now the Christian Democrats are gonna walk in and take over."

"What do we do now?" they asked the young consultants.

The first thing Kelly Kimball thought was, "Wow. This is something I understand. I'm here, and I can help."

The second thing he thought was, "My God, if I can help, they're in really bad shape."

What the people eagerly pumping their guests for information likely did not understand was that this was the big leagues for their visitors. The sort of things they were discussing were the province of senior presidential campaign managers, not of direct-democracy guys or direct-mail specialists. The Americans were profoundly aware of their own limited expertise. They knew strategies that worked in California, Ohio, or Indiana. Not in Eastern Europe.

The Slovaks were too fresh and young and naïve to think like that. Or maybe just too desperate. Thanks to the decades of Soviet control, there was no democratic political expertise in Eastern Europe at all. In the land of the blind, the one-eyed visitors were kings and queens.

The Slovaks were eager to talk about politics, politics, and more politics. Even when it turned out that much of what the visitors had to say had limited application to a Czechoslovakian situation they did not really understand.

When the guests brought up get-out-the-vote efforts they thought might interest their audience, they met an almost total rejection. There were too many unsettling parallels between typical efforts to rally democratic support at home and the apparatus the Soviets used to maintain a totalitarian state. Compiling voter lists was much like communist bureaucracy. Knocking on doors to talk to voters about policies was even less popular. "No one knocks on doors here. That's what the communists used to do." The idea of putting people in a minivan to drive them to the poll was simply unthinkable.

Under the communists, if someone put you in a minivan, there was a good chance you wouldn't come back.

The people behind VPN clearly had organizational skills.

Before and during the Velvet Revolution, they had been able to draw thousands of demonstrators to protest in the main square under threat of jail and violence. But until now, they had been a movement. They had united everyone outside the mainstream who was against the communists.

That was a lot of people.

Now, the political consultants tried to explain, they had to become a party.

They had to stop being against something and start being for something.

They had to have a strategy, policies, and plans. They needed a face and a message. They needed issues and solutions. They had to be strategic about their messaging. They had to show people that they had a long-term plan for governing.

They had to find a different skill set.

From spearheading the protest against the communist government, it was a mighty flip to turn around and say, "OK, now we are the government. And now we've got to convince the same people who were anti-everything to become pro-government."

That night, the Slovak politicians were oblivious to what lay ahead of them, and what it would mean for the people in the room. They weren't aware of the looming threat to the friendships they had made. They didn't know how organizations fall apart when power becomes real.

Or what it would ultimately do to their country.

For now, they were looking to the Americans for answers. For the Americans, it felt like being approached by George Washington for advice during the winter at Valley Forge, if only on where to find firewood.

Kimball found it inspirational, but he wasn't disappointed to be moving on the next morning.

If they stuck around, they might screw things up.

Democracy was something their new friends would have died for—they had risked death for—the guests fell in love with their hosts because of the remarkable stories they told about what they had gone through just to get to that point. It was just overwhelming. The visitors got torn up by emotional accounts of families being torn apart and people going to jail for demonstrating.

They were overwhelmed by the honesty and passion. They wanted to help.

No one wanted to stop talking, so they carried on until 4:00 a.m.

The newcomers were excited to spark conversations with their ideas and suggestions.

Most of the strategies they put forward wouldn't and couldn't work in Slovakia, but that didn't matter. US strategy was still better than no strategy at all. To that extent, the visitors introduced VPN to a different way of thinking that started with a strategy.

It was humbling to explain to someone with experience of living under Soviet rule how the Republicans and Democrats used their differences as the basis for election campaigns at home. In the eyes of the Europeans, politics was a continuum, with communists at one end and fascists at the other. On their continuum, Republicans and Democrats fit into exactly the same place. Even the young political operators had to admit that US elections didn't make much real change. The stability of the US system and the federal–state balance means that any changes were small.

It was, they conceded, both a strength and a weakness of the system.

To be thrown into the middle of an actual revolution was

a different order of things. To meet the people who put their lives on the line to bring down a government and break up the Eastern Bloc. It turned out that the kind of people who were prepared to do that, to go to prison and put their families at risk, looked just like them. None of the North Americans knew any politicians like that.

They had heard about it. They had seen it in movies. They read it in the press. But you rarely get to meet people like that.

And even more rarely do they ask for your advice.

THE EVENING ENDS

No one wanted to stop talking, but the evening finally ended at about 4:00 a.m. A few hours later, the Americans were out of there. With some regret, but mainly with big hangovers.

They boarded a bus for what turned out to be an eventful journey to Prague. Most thought that was the end of the story—but that was not the case.

Because a few hours after they set out for Prague, a group of equally hungover leaders of VPN set out in their cars to follow them.

They wanted to get their consultants back.

They wanted to continue the conversation.

Hungarian activists, veterans of the last free Parliamentary election, prepare to participate in the Campaigns & Elections workshop in Budapest.

James Dwinell (standing, right) talks to Carl Gershman, President of National Endowment for Democracy at lunch in the VPN offices in Bratislava; (left to right): Ján Budaj, interpreter, Gordy Robson, Christine LaPalle, Jennifer Laszlo Mizrahi. Andrew Frank is in the background.

Jan Budaj

Verjnost Proti Nasiliu (VPM)
Koordinacny Vydor
Jiraskova 10, 813 36
Bratislava, Czechoslovakia

Fax   011-42 7 330313

Ján Budaj's "business card"

Ján Budaj standing with interpreter in the VPN offices in Bratislava. (Seated, left to right): Fedor Gál, Gordy Robson, Carl Gershman, and Andrew Frank.

James Dwinell addresses the seminar in Bratislava.

Scenes from Bratislava.

Andrew Frank (center) in Bratislava with (left to right): Anton Mrazek (Frank's host), Juraj Mihalik, Iveta Mrazekova (Anton's wife), and Tanya Mihalikova.

(Left to right): Barry Fadem, Kelly Kimball, Ginny Kotnick, Greg Lyle, and Trish Whitcomb, captured live in a Prague hotel room.

Juraj Mikalik (left), our main contact with VPN, meets with Kelly Kimball and Barry Fadem at a pub in Prague.

Trish Whitcomb takes time out to enjoy an ice cream cone in Wenceslas Square in Prague before heading back to Bratislava to work with VPN.

C&E speakers take a tour of Prague; Phil Noble is the tall man in center.

Gordy Robson addresses the audience at the seminar in Warsaw.

Kelly Kimball (center) enjoys dinner with several of his C&E colleagues.

Participants in the C&E seminars in Warsaw. (Seated, left to right): James Dwinell, Polish host, and Gordy Robson; (standing, far left): Jennifer Mizrahi and Andrew Frank; (back row, right of center): Kelly Kimball.

WEST MEETS EAST

Drawn by pure democracy, consultants are reborn in Eastern Europe, by James David Barber

At the invitation of numerous emerging political parties in Czechoslovakia, Poland, and Hungary, Campaigns & Elections exported its campaign training seminars to Eastern Europe for sessions March 6-16. One of the participants, James David Barber, was the designated scribe. This is his report.

We arrived as humble teachers. We left as activist allies, anxious to help make democracy—real democracy—happen in Eastern Europe.

Our conscience was off limits. We didn't come to preach at the democratic converts like some pontificating patriarch who drops in to straighten out his children. From the start, as our Canadian leader Gordon Robson put it, we were not in Hungary, Czechoslovakia, and Poland to instruct them on how to imitate us. Our American leader, Campaigns & Elections publisher James Dwinell, echoed Robson's sentiments when he said, "We are not here to teach but to learn. We will show you our ways but as with a menu, you need to choose the tactics and strategies that are right for you and your political culture and teach us."

We came stressing cool tolerance and open mindedness, and listened for their special needs and concerns. As Florida-based consultant Lee Miller put it, "We offered you hammers and nails."

We whirled around, spending a few days in each country, working seminars which started out sparsely populated in Budapest, and ended in Warsaw with more than 350 political party officials attending. On the way, we changed. We fell off the teacher's stool and took up the flag of freedom. We planed back to America eager to help democracy grow from the revolution.

There were surprises that awakened our jaded band. For instance, is there anything more vital to a campaign than lists of voters? Last fall, Hungary did a major national referendum, a vote which decided to delay the choice of a president until the new parliament was elected. Surely anyone gearing up for a parliamentary election would want that referendum list specifying thousands of available voters. But to Hungarians, person-listing had been a weapon of the secret police for more than four decades. Tear them up and throw them away, they said.

We thought the rock-bottom challenge of political journalism is going to be how to write the story. But over there, the biggest challenge is getting paper to print the story on. In Poland, the Communists bill their own newspapers 800 zlotys (about 8 cents) for a section of paper. Solidarity, the democracy movement, is charged 5,000 zlotys, per section. In Eastern Europe, newspapers are powerful campaign tools, not forums for unbiased reporting.

And, we thought, if you're running for office, surely you'd like to get your spouse on television or in the newspaper. But to them, that implies nepotism—that if you win, your spouse will get a special job.

The political scene in Eastern Europe is different from that in Eastern New Jersey. As Wayne Johnson observed, "We argue about zoning. They're deciding whether or not to legalize private property."

The upcoming elections are not like our 1988 model. They are more like 1788, when our democracy was being constituted in its basic fundamentals. Tony Quinn may be right in suggesting that "maybe we should encourage them to think of [Vaclav] Havel and [Lech] Walesa as

playing the role of a Washington or DeGaulle as they get underway."

Argentinian pollster Felipe Noguera has it right when he says that "these countries are not just going though a change of administration, but of regime."

In Hungary we were scheduled to seminar in "Karl Marx University." By the time we got there, the name had been changed to "University of Economics of Budapest."

The big news from the three nations we visited is that democracy has stepped out onto the high wire, leaving behind the rigid communist platform, facing forward to a risky chance to establish freedom and justice for all. Now is the hour to guarantee non violence, citizenship for all, rational consent of the governed, genuine law to regulate the

Democracy comes to Wenceslas Square, Prague

economy and society, and secure, democratically controlled foreign relations.

But to make it happen, leadership is necessary. In Hungary there is a revulsion against coming out for some new political star. In Czechoslovakia, the opposite occurred. The love for Havel, the playwright-president, is almost universal.

April - May, 1990 / Page 17

In Poland, Solidarity leader Lech Walesa has increasingly quiet respect, as if he were becoming yesterday's leader.

More importantly, what's needed is local leadership, from the village on up. In Poland, they need thousands of candidates for local and regional offices before the June election, an event unknown since World War II.

Political parties have been born, but they have yet to pass through their identity crisis. Solidarity started as a trade union and is now an umbrella for all sorts of parties. As a Solidarity M.P. put it, "What unifies us is the will to fight the communists." But with the communists on the way out, Solidarity must begin to organize national unity.

Hungary, on the other hand, lacks a national umbrella. The Czechs have a broad-based "Civic Forum" and the Slovaks the rapidly broadening "Public Against Violence." When our professional consultants talked about how to build

VEREJNOSŤ PROTI NÁSILIU

The Slovak organization "Public Against Violence" has become an umbrella for smaller Czech parties

coalitions, eyes lit up. A new version of the Federalist Papers might make a hit.

Media politics is on a roll, but wobbling. Christine LaPaille says that "as democracy emerges in these countries, the press will emerge also." But virtually all the radio, television, and newspaper facilities are owned by the state. Harsh censors at the top have been replaced by permissive editors and producers. Reporters on the street are inventing their journalism day by day.

Democracy rests on citizens, which is why *Campaigns & Elections'* seminars centered on the age-old questions of democracy. How do you activate voters? Where do you get money to buy the tools for campaign action?

As the long days went on, those of us who listened and looked began to experience a newness of life. When you have lunch with an aging fellow working hard in politics after being jailed for six years as a political prisoner; when you have

supper with a beautiful 17-year-old gypsy girl who is emerging as a vivid volunteer among many who think a gypsy is an animal; when you breakfast with a reporter whose weekly magazine was underground and now going public; or you walk the street with a woman translator about to have a third child, who says she never joined the communists because "you have to look your children in the eye;" those happenings turn your mind.

Randy Gilliland, president of Gilliland & Co., a fundraising firm, put it this way: "After spending many years in the American political arena, I had grown cynical. I had tired of petty political arguments and in many ways lost my sense of political vision and idealism. This trip invigorated me. It made me turn back to the dreams and idealistic views of my younger years."

Such renewed dreams are sparking realities: Gilliland and Wayne Johnson are raising funds for six East European political organizations, working to get U.S. newspapers to support papers in Poland, and trying to have equipment contributed to party offices.

Lee Miller, has taken on projects in two countries for "organizational and communications opportunities."

C&E'S EASTERN EUROPE FACULTY

Chuck Adams
Adams and Co., Salem, OR

James David Barber
Duke University, Durham, NC

Robin Bell
International Center for Development Policy, Washington, DC

Scott Berkowitz
C&E, Washington, DC

Graham Bruce, M.L.A.
Government of British Columbia, Duncan, BC

James Dwinell
C&E, Washington, DC

Barry Fadem
Bagatelos & Fadem, San Francisco, CA

Andrew Frank
C&E, Washington, DC

George Gibault
Public Affairs Bureau, Victoria, BC

Randy Gilliland
Gilliland & Company, Midlothian, VA

Sal Guzzetta
Political Publishing, Alexandria, VA

Wayne Johnson
Wayne C. Johnson & Assoc., Sacramento, CA

Jennifer Kessler
C&E, Washington, DC

Kelly Kimball
Kimball Petition Management West Los Angeles, CA

Ginnie Kontnik
Harriman Communications Center Washington, DC

Jerry Lampert
Principal Secretary to the Premier Victoria, BC

Christine LaPaille
Agenda Communications Chicago, IL

Greg Lyle
Principal Secretary to the Premier of Manitoba, Winnipeg, Manitoba

Lindsay Mattison
International Center for Development Policy, Washington, DC

Lee Miller
Miller Consulting Group, Ltd. Fort Lauderdale, FL

George Gibault, director of research for the Public Affairs Bureau in British Columbia, linked himself to numerous agricultural enterprises, whose technical aid he will enlist for urgent training needs.

A stunning conversion from preaching to participating happened when Ginnie Kontnik, director of Harriman Communications Center in Washington, and professional consultants Kelly Kimball, Trish Whitcomb, Barry Fadem, and Grey Lyle struggled all night with "Public Against Violence," the major organization working for democracy in the Slovakia part of Czechoslovakia.

Kontnik and the rest see themselves as "volunteers who were asked to help." And help they will. They have formed the nonprofit volunteers for democracy to get donations of high-tech equipment and a supply of detailed strategic advice. The group already has put together a set of four-minute television ads for Public Against Violence to be used

Collecting political party volunteers in Wenceslas Square, Prague

daily from April until the June election. The first one tells the Czech voter: "VPN took you to the revolution in Wenceslas Square. Vote on the ballot so we can finish the revolution!"

To finish the revolution is to found democracy. In the capitol of Poland, we visited the great hall of the national parliament. Up front, facing the elected representatives, is the symbol of Poland, a white eagle with outstretched wings. The communists left the eagle there in 1945, but smashed the crown off its head. When we were there, workers were putting on a new crown. Will the new crown of democracy hold firm on the head of the nation? The wonder and the uncertainty are still there. ❏

James David Barber is on the faculty of Duke University in North Carolina as a James B. Duke Professor of Political Science and Policy Studies.

Rev. James Noble
Decatur, GA
Phil Noble
The Palmetto Project, Charleston, SC
Felipe Noguera
Mora y Araujo Noguera,
Buenos Aires, Argentina
Beth Provinse
Conotabs, Bethesda, MD
Tony Quinn
Braun and Company
Sacramento, CA
Gianni Riotta
Corriere Della Sera, New York, NY
Gordon Robson
Robson and Assoc., Maple Ridge, BC
Mary Robson,
Robson and Assoc., Maple Ridge, BC

Cliff Scotton
New Democratic Party of Canada,
Nanaimo, BC
Amanda Smith
Sex Equity Consultant, Durham, NC
Patricia Whitcomb
Bates & Associates, Indianapolis, IN
Robert White
International Center for
Development Policy, Washington, DC

VOLUNTEERS FOR DEMOCRACY

Several participants in C&E's trip have formed a non-profit organization to provide support for VPN, the Slovak Democracy movement. If you would like to donate computers, faxes, copiers, your time, or anything else, please call (800) 237-7842.

The post-trip summary article in C&E, listing the names of all participants and mentioning Volunteers For Democracy.

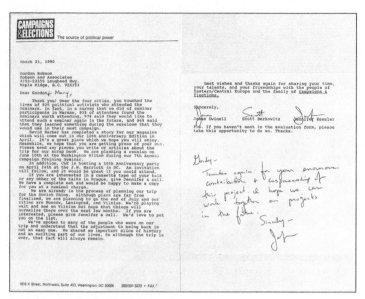

Letter from C&E thanking Gordy Robson for his participation in the trip.

Andrew Frank and VPN leader Milan Knaszko, a famous former actor in Czechoslovakia.

Andrew Frank and Anton Mrazek on a visit to Vienna to pick up supplies.

Poster with the logo of VPN.

CHAPTER 4

PRAGUE

EVEN BEFORE THE VPN LEADERS FOLLOWED THE C&E tour to Prague, the wheels had come off. Or, more accurately, the roof had come off. Literally.

Prague was one of the heartlands of Eastern Europe's recovery from Soviet control, led by the charismatic Václav Havel, who had become interim president in December 1989. The city was already on the tourist map for young French and German kids. Czech politics had gotten a lot of attention from the United States, and the NDI, the IRI, and the NED were all represented in the capital, ready to give advice to Havel's Civic Forum.

For all that, Westerners were still a novelty for most Czechs.

When Andrew Frank had arrived late at night on his original scouting trip to the city, he found hardly anybody at the airport. As usual, he had few set plans, but he met a man who spoke some English who asked where Frank was heading. Despite Frank's misgivings, the man turned out not to be a hustler but merely someone who jumped at the chance to hang out with an American. The guy gave Frank a ride to a traditional beer hall in downtown Prague and then explained that there was a hotel across the street, which is where Frank stayed after a few drinks.

The stranger's euphoria at feeling that the country was swinging to face the West was palpable. And gracious. It was the most striking welcome Frank received in Eastern Europe.

The next day, Frank met his translator. Her family was old Prague, who had to leave when they had problems during the war. He got the feeling from how she talked they were probably Jewish. That interested him because, in each country he traveled, he explored what survived of their Jewish heritage. It was a family thing, members of his parents' families having emigrated to the United States from German in the mid-1800s and around the turn of the twentieth century because of pogroms from Russia, Ukraine, and Sered in the Austro-Hungarian Empire (now in Slovakia).

When the C&E staff arrived, they found the Czechs difficult to get accustomed to. James Dwinell met with the organizers of the event in a small, semi-underground theater and explained what they were doing there. He talked a little and then waited for the translator to repeat what he had said. She said nothing. Dwinell looked at her until she rolled her eyes and explained, "They don't need to know that." Then he talked for another thirty or forty-five seconds and waited. Again, silence. Dwinell waited some more. Eventually, the woman said, "They already know that."

To Dwinell, that just came across as arrogance.

It went some way to explaining the Slovaks' resentment of the Czechs' belief that they were somehow superior and the thoughts of independence it encouraged.

One of the things that struck the North Americans most was the realization of how many times they said the word "check." Only now, it induced gales of laughter.

Not that anyone could speak Czech. They spoke English very slowly and quite loudly for the benefit of the foreigners.

FLASHBACK

The main C&E party arrived in Prague under a cloud.

For Kelly Kimball, Barry Fadem, and Trish Whitcomb, it was the result of a five-hour bus ride with a hangover from the night at Juraj's apartment. For the others, it was the result of having to listen to Olga.

The bus seemed at least fifty years old and would have been uncomfortable even without the hangovers Kelly Kimball, Barry Fadem, and Trish Whitcomb were nursing from the long evening at Juraj's apartment. The ride to Prague was only about 200 miles, but it took five hours. Thanks to Olga, thought Kimball, it felt at least twice as long.

Olga was the guide the Czech government had assigned to the party from C&E. She was a matronly woman of four feet-seven inches who everyone agreed had probably had something to do with the secret police—and who still might have.

As the bus pulled away from the hotel in Bratislava, Olga started talking on the microphone from where she sat up front next to the driver, Igor. After a while, Kimball started to wonder when she would stop talking. After a little longer, he realized that she didn't intend to stop talking until they arrived in Prague. She seemed to be providing not so much a running commentary on the places they were passing as an account of Czech history. Which was very, very long. In Olga's story, the Russians were the big brothers from the East who had done so much to help Czechoslovakia.

"Give me strength," Kimball muttered to Barry Fadem, who was sitting very quietly next to him. "Is this going to go on through the whole trip?" Fadem didn't say anything. They both already knew the answer.

Olga and Igor were both straight out of central casting, with comedy stereotypical names and appearances. Igor loved his bus, and Olga loved her country. In fact, Olga turned out to love the former version of her country quite a lot more than the current version because she decided to tell the busload of experts on campaigns and elections that she had no great love of democracy.

At one part of the journey, Olga spelled out why she herself would not even be voting in the upcoming elections. Politicians, she said, promised everything and then never came through with any of their promises. Which, given that there hadn't been freely elected politicians in Czechoslovakia for decades, wasn't a view based on much personal experience.

It was like listening to a central Communist Party description of the shortcomings of democracy—and delivered in a monotonous tone best described as unexcited but intensely earnest. If that was the normal mode of bus entertainment in Eastern Europe, it was no wonder the Soviet Union was breaking up, reflected Kimball.

Nowadays, he'd have put on some noise-canceling headphones. Back then, the only way to stop the sound would have been to put his fingers in his ears. Instead, he thought about the people he had met the previous evening.

The thought of the excitement in Juraj's apartment was a useful counterpoint to Olga's droning cynicism. Before she had even had a chance to vote for the first time in her life, Olga had decided that the whole election was pointless. She thought that politics were a waste of time.

For Kimball, in contrast, it seemed like he was closer to politics that would really make a difference than at any time in his career.

After a couple of hours, when the bus was out on the highway, passing through the countryside, Olga eventually shut up. There remained a danger that she was only catching her breath, so Kimball decided to use the opportunity to try to catch up on some sleep.

He was just nodding off when he was jolted awake by a popping sound as loud as an explosion.

"Jeez, what was that?" he said to Fadem, who was looking in alarm toward the back of the bus. Kimball followed his friend's eyes and turned just in time to see the back part of the roof shake violently and start to lift up from the rest of the bus. It seemed to hover in place for a moment, then the wind caught it and lifted it clear into the air, ripping it off the sides of the bus. It sailed up and then crashed down out of sight. A blare of horns from behind them confirmed that it had landed on the highway.

On the bus, there were gasps and a few stifled screams. Anyone who had been dozing was wide awake, grasping hard to the edges of their seats in case any more of the bus was about to rattle off. People looked at each other in panic in the way Kimball imagined airplane travelers would look if the oxygen masks suddenly dropped from the ceiling.

As the wind swirled around the exposed passengers, whipping up their hair, Igor jammed on his brakes and pulled the bus over to the side of the road. They sat in stunned silence for a moment, though Kimball was pretty sure no one was actually hurt.

"What the hell happened?" he asked Fadem. Everyone on the bus was asking the same thing.

Fadem said, "I don't know. I think some guy was playing with the emergency exit."

The same conclusion seemed to have been reached by Igor, who had gotten out of the bus to look behind at part of his pride and joy lying on the highway, and who had now climbed back onboard to shout at his passengers. You didn't need to speak Czech to tell that the guy was pissed. Really pissed. He was shouting at everyone in general, but more specifically, berating people in a handful of seats, clearly demanding to know who was responsible.

Everyone kept quiet. No one was going to admit anything in the face of the driver's rage.

Now Olga reinforced her secret police credentials by stepping in to calm Igor down. He stopped shouting, and she spoke to him quietly for a while. He glared at his passengers, then went to sit back down in the driver's seat.

Olga drew herself up to her full height, which was not very tall, and addressed the passengers. "Someone tried to open the emergency door. That is not allowed. Now the roof is broken. It must be paid for."

Kimball and Fadem looked at each other and couldn't help themselves from starting to grin at the absurdity of the situation.

They grinned a bit less when Olga said, "Until we know who is responsible, you must all surrender your passports." There was a murmur of dissent around the passengers. They all knew nightmare stories about totalitarian states taking away passports. But Olga made it perfectly clear that Igor was not going any further until everyone had given up their passports. Igor himself made it even more clear, sitting in his seat like a child in a tantrum.

Olga began walking through the bus collecting the passports. And suddenly there they were: a bunch of representatives of democratic politics in the middle of a former communist country with no means to prove their identity, and no way to leave the country.

Igor pulled the bus back onto the road, and the wind started to whip through the passengers' hair. It wasn't comfortable. Kimball gave up on any chance of sleep, although he did also note with relief that Olga's commentary had come to an end. Perhaps the speakers had been on the part of the roof that blew away. As they drove along, the story of what had actually happened circulated in whispers so that the Czechs didn't hear them.

The C&E rule was that there was no smoking on shared transportation like buses. But one of the tourists, Lindsay Mattison of the International Center for Development Policy in Washington DC, was a chain smoker. He couldn't or wouldn't control himself. He was so desperate for a cigarette that he opened what he thought was a vent or window at the top of the bus so he could get rid of the smoke. The catch he pulled turned out to be the release for the emergency exit. The top of the coach popped up and was caught in the wind, which ripped it off like the top of a can.

Though as they drove along with their rather primitive air conditioning, it seemed from what Kimball could overhear that Mattison was blaming everyone else for the incident rather than himself.

CITY OF COOL

The visitors found Prague bigger, more beautiful, more lively, and more Westernized than Bratislava.

Bratislava and its buildings reflected Soviet sensibility; austerity for workers, and preservation of beautiful, historic structures for the pleasures of the ruling class. It was like a factory town.

Prague was a city of ice cream and Frank Zappa and young French and German backpackers and trolley cars, and romance. At the Charles Bridge across the river, everyone fixed padlocks to the railings as a symbol of lasting love. Eventually, the weight of the locks threatened to make the bridge collapse.

Much of the city looked like Disney World because its buildings were so well-preserved and so old. Some cobblestone streets had been built in the 1500s.

The C&E party stayed at the Alcron, a beautiful old hotel with a sweeping staircase and threadbare Art Deco glamour. To put it briefly, Prague was cool.

ALL POLITICS IS LOCAL

The seminars in Prague were the best of the whole trip, with the speakers having honed their message and an audience so large they had to have breakout rooms. Andrew Frank, who was already leaving for Warsaw, was pleased with the attendance. So were his bosses.

Trish Whitcomb teamed up with Wayne Johnson to talk about direct mail but immediately ran into similar difficulties she had found in Bratislava. No one wanted to give their data to anyone they didn't have to. Everyone told her, "We don't do that because that's what the communists do."

That was back in the days when people had a concern with data privacy that seems almost quaint now.

Barry Fadem, meanwhile, started his slot with Kelly Kimball by saying, "Obviously, Kelly and I were not around for the American Revolution, but I can't tell you how proud we are to be here today for your revolution. Prague is the birthplace of democracy in Eastern Europe."

The place went nuts. He got a standing ovation. After Fadem went missing in Prague the next day, Kimball tried the same line on his own in Warsaw. It didn't get the same welcome.

For Phil Noble, the Czech Republic was different from the rest of Eastern Europe. He had been there in 1972 as a hitchhiker, and he was aware of its democratic tradition that went way back. Philosophers and activists crafted Charter 77 in Prague in 1976. Under Slovak leader Alexander Dubček, Czechoslovakia again challenged communism in what became known as the Prague Spring in 1968. Charter 77 was a civic resolution to challenge communist power. The Prague Spring showed emboldened protests to the world. It was as if the communists had never managed to extinguish democracy. Despite suppressing it, they had never quite extinguished the flame. The Czechs simply wouldn't let them.

On his previous trip, Phil Noble had come across the communist bureaucracy. He had observed that the rules and the regulations were not discussable and non-negotiable. Everybody stayed within the process. But if you just jumped outside the rules and didn't pay attention to them, no one knew how to deal with you. As a hitchhiker, he was picked up all the time by the police. At the police station, he'd watch them arguing about the rules, saying, "There's nothing in the book that says foreigners can't hitchhike," because they didn't get any foreign visitors anyway.

At one stage, Noble was picked up by a schoolteacher and spent the night at his home. The schoolteacher took him to the barn and brushed away some hay to reveal twenty-five or thirty books. Noble didn't know what the books were, but the teacher told him, "We still read these banned books. I share them with my friends."

The Czechs had a tradition of dissent that the other countries didn't. Noble's father, the Reverend Noble, had told him about Jan Hus, who led the Protestant reformation there in the fifteenth century. Hus was the Czechs' own Martin Luther. They had their own tradition of reforming, of rebellion, of independence that the other countries didn't have.

Dr. James Noble had connections among preachers in Czechoslovakia and had been in contact with them for a while. At one stage, he took his son to visit a Czech preacher in Prague. They talked about the start of the Velvet Revolution and how people had turned up in the square to demonstrate Sunday after Sunday.

The number of people who turned out was steady for weeks before all of a sudden, it jumped, and suddenly hundreds of thousands of people were showing up. The Nobles wondered why. The preacher told them it was because the demonstrations were covered on the news, and the TV audience realized that the protestors weren't getting shot. So everyone watching the news thought, we can go out now, and they won't shoot us. Within the next couple of days, the preacher was talking about it to his congregation and saying, "Folks, we can do this. We can go out and do something, and they won't call out the troops." That's how it escalated.

Communist control was falling apart. The guys in Prague were turning to the Soviets for marching orders, and nobody in Moscow was picking up the phone. The Russians were too busy trying to take care of their own problems, and they just left them alone. Over and over, the visitors heard the phrase, "I turned to Moscow for instructions, and nobody answered the phone."

So the Czechs were in the streets, and their politicians had to respond in some way. They would do so without the Communist Party telling them what to do.

Czech politics were in Czech hands. As former US Speaker

of the House, Tip O'Neil, once said, "At the end of the day, all politics is local."

FLASHBACK

The morning had gone pretty well, thought Scott Berkowitz in Prague. The workshops were well attended. The week was coming to a satisfactory conclusion. But there was a doubt nagging at the back of his mind: "How are we going to get home without our passports?"

He looked at the people holding the workshops—people for whose welfare he was responsible. He hadn't told them about the passports because he didn't want to worry them. But he was worried. The way the passports had been gathered up and spirited away without explanation was a stark reminder of the power of the old communist bureaucracy. It made it seem like they were a long way from home.

He didn't notice exactly when Olga appeared in the room. But there she was, beyond the seated delegates, talking to one of the other speakers, who turned and pointed to Scott. "Oh God, she's coming this way." Berkowitz was desperate not to betray his rising anxiety, so he smiled and said good morning.

Olga said to him, "Will you please come with me?"

Berkowitz followed her out of the room, remembering to smile and nod to his colleagues. Perhaps she just wanted to talk somewhere more private outside the room. But when they got outside, she kept walking down the stairs and across the lobby. Berkowitz suddenly realized that they were heading outside, and his mind started to fill with dread. Just then, he saw Trish Whitcomb walking into the building.

He said, "If I'm not back in an hour, please tell James that Olga has me."

Olga did have him. He'd always assumed that at least part of the guide's job was to keep tabs on the visitors, so she was probably former secret police. And now she was less guide and more guard.

"Where are we going?" Berkowitz asked, but Olga was not in the mood for a chat as she led him through a maze of streets. "God, is she pissed," thought the American.

Eventually, they got to a large, anonymous building, and Olga marched through the door. "What is this place? Where are we?" Berkowitz asked.

Olga said sternly, "This is the Ministry of Buses."

What the hell? Things were getting a bit more ominous. Berkowitz was an optimistic character, but this was all starting to feel a bit Kafkaesque.

They went into the building, and it was like walking into an Escher engraving as they went up three flights of stairs, around a hallway, a couple of turns back down a flight of stairs, then along a corridor and back around to the back of the building before they went up another two flights of stairs. It occurred to the American that Olga might be lost, but she strode on through an endless maze of corridors. It felt to him that they had been walking for hours, although it was probably only fifteen minutes. The Ministry of Buses was a pretty big deal. Berkowitz wondered where on earth they were headed.

Wherever it was, they had arrived. Olga opened a door and showed him in. It was a tiny room with no windows and concrete walls. "You will wait here," said Olga, with what Berkowitz suspected was a little hint of satisfaction. Olga left and closed the door behind her. For form's sake, Berkowitz tried the handle, although he already knew what he'd discover. It was locked, and it couldn't be opened from the inside.

He was effectively in a cell. There were no circumstances in which that could be good news.

Berkowitz sat down on the only chair to wait. He started to run through his options in his head, but that didn't take long because he didn't have any. The minutes passed, and as he gazed at the walls and waited, he started to feel less nervous and a bit more pissed. Why was he here when he should be doing his job back at the workshops? It felt like he was being deliberately intimidated, and that sucked.

After what felt like hours—he never found out how long it actually was—the door opened and a man in a suit and tie came into the room. He shut the door behind him and started speaking in halting English. He pointed to his own chest and said, "I am deputy minister of buses." Then he pointed at Berkowitz and said some more things, of which the only one the American could make out was, "You broke the bus, you pay for the bus."

After a couple of dozen words, the deputy minister's knowledge of English ran out. Berkowitz's knowledge of Czech didn't even reach those heights, so he simply looked at the man and shook his head.

The deputy minister asked him for $80,000 to pay for the bus.

"Sure, I got that right here." It was a ludicrous price for a bus that already seemed at least fifty years old. Berkowitz shook his head some more.

The deputy minister spoke a lot in Czech before suggesting a sum of $60,000.

Not knowing what to say—and not able to say it in Czech anyway—Berkowitz said, "You must be joking," and shook his head again.

The deputy minister was getting pissed. His voice was getting a little louder. He argued for a while—all lost on Berkowitz—and then suggested $50,000. The American still insisted that it was too much.

The two men kept arguing back and forth, each getting

increasingly angry until, finally, the deputy minister reached the sum of $30,000. Before Berkowitz could even get around to rejecting the figure again, the deputy minister had stormed out of the room, slamming the door shut behind him.

The young American wondered what would happen now. He knew one thing that wasn't going to happen: he wasn't going to pay anyone $30,000. Simply put, he couldn't.

A half hour later, the door opened, and Olga said, "Let's go." She walked him back through the mazelike building, and Berkowitz realized that he had been there all afternoon, as it was now near the end of the day. She took him back to the hotel without much conversation.

Berkowitz was feeling bruised by his afternoon, and he suspected that Olga might also not have had the most pleasant of experiences in the Ministry of Buses. He asked her, "Um, what happens now?"

"I will let you know."

"Can we have our passports back?"

"No, I have them."

That evening, the former US ambassador to El Salvador arrived. He wasn't part of the trip but he now ran the think tank that employed the guy who had actually pulled the lever that released the top of the bus. He showed up to get his man out of any trouble. He found Berkowitz and said, "I need his passport."

Berkowitz replied, "Well, there's not much I can do about that right now."

"But we're supposed to leave early tomorrow morning, so I really need it."

Well, because even a former US ambassador is a pretty big deal, Berkowitz went and found Olga. He didn't want to have to beg—but he begged. He begged, and because a former US ambassador is a pretty big deal, Olga eventually reluctantly handed over the passport of the one person who was more to blame for the incident than anyone else. As Berkowitz handed it over, he couldn't help reflecting on the fact that while he'd spent the afternoon incarcerated in the Ministry of Buses, the culprit was getting off scot-free. And everyone else was stuck.

Berkowitz had an uneasy night. It wasn't clear what was going to happen, but C&E couldn't afford to pay $30,000—nor could he. This had all the makings of an international diplomatic incident.

Especially when the US Embassy in Prague called to find out what was going on. (An unexpected byproduct of the crisis was an invitation to the entire C&E party to go on a forty-five-minute tour of the embassy, which everyone enjoyed, even if the then-ambassador, Shirley Temple, was absent.)

Most of the party was still happily unaware of Berkowitz's ordeal the previous afternoon or of the uncertainty with which he got ready to check his charges out ready to head to the airport—still without the passports.

When he got to the desk he found that the $30,000 charge for the bus had been added to his bill. He looked at the hotel manager, who looked nervously back, having simply been ordered to put the bus on the bill. Scott shook his head, pointed at the line item, and started repeating exactly the same argument he had had the previous afternoon, only this time with someone who could speak English.

This time, it only took an hour to negotiate the manager down to $2,000, which Berkowitz said he could pay at once. The manager agreed that that was surely enough to fix a fifty-year old bus. So, more surprisingly, did Olga, who turned up with their passports just as the party were preparing to leave the hotel.

On the surface, Scott Berkowitz remained swanlike and

serene. Under the water, he was paddling like crazy. But sud-
denly, they were on another bus headed for the airport, and he
realized that he might have been barely holding things together
for the last two weeks—but he had pulled it off.

LUNCH MEETING

When Trish Whitcomb bumped into Scott Berkowitz and Olga as they left the seminars, she was heading out for lunch. She ate wild boar, the official state dish of Czechoslovakia, with a member of the interim parliament. The MP's father was an engineer and his mother a chemist, and their status as scientists gave them certain privileges, among which was a television and free schooling. They rejected the privileges, especially the television, because they did not want to be beholden to the state. Instead, they chose to homeschool their son, who was in any case able eventually to go to university in Prague, where he completed a PhD in physics. It was only after further study in Germany and acquiring another PhD, that he decided to come back to serve in the parliament.

What struck Trish Whitcomb was the reason he had chosen his academic path. He felt that he wanted to do something meaningful but not something that would be tainted by any kind of political philosophy. He decided on physics because he believed that its laws were laws: they were not open to interpretation.

For someone as committed to politics as Trish Whitcomb, it was a remarkable display of commitment to objectivity.

UNEXPECTED VISITORS

As it happened, that would be Trish's last day with the C&E

group, because later on the VPN representatives showed up in Prague.

Kelly Kimball took a call in his room from the ambassador's residence. The VPN had reached out to the embassy to find out how to reach the touring group. The embassy was taken a little off guard. When he answered, an American voice asked him, "Why are the government of Slovakia here, asking for you? And, by the way, Who the **** are you?"

It came as a surprise to Kimball. Not so much that the Slovakians were there, but learning who they actually were. The previous night he had been under the impression that they had been a random group of people who went to the square to protest against the communists. Not an effective government.

Juraj came on the line and asked, "Where are you guys? We're looking for you."

Kimball went to find Barry Fadem in his room. He said, "The US embassy has been on the phone."

Fadem said, "You spoke to Shirley Temple? Did she sing 'On the Good Ship Lollipop?'"

"No, not her, some other dude. Anyway, the VPN people from last night are here."

"Where?"

"Here, in Prague. They want to meet us."

Kimball and Fadem walked through Wenceslas Square to meet the Slovaks. The square was the epicenter, ground zero. It was where the Velvet Revolution had started and in many ways where it was still going on. As the two friends walked through that night on the way to meet the Slovaks, it was full of activity.

The whole place was in transition. It really did feel as if they'd been spirited into the middle of a revolution.

The members of VPN who turned up in Prague included

Juraj and his gracious wife Tanya, a laid-back woman who had helped him build his business and who kept a lot of their friends together. After the unity of VPN during the revolution splintered into bitter division, she became very defensive of her husband after she decided that many of their friends had become selfish and destructive.

Kimball and Fadem led VPN back to the hotel's subterranean bar to meet with Trish Whitcomb. They talked and drank Russian champagne—it was as bad as it sounded—and they came up with a tentative plan.

There wasn't much time. The main C&E group was due to leave the next day. Andrew Frank had already left. But they agreed that Barry Fadem would stay behind in Prague to talk to the VPN about a constitution, and Trish Whitcomb would go back to Bratislava and talk more to people there about organizing for a campaign.

"I'll meet you in Warsaw," Fadem said to Kimball. This came as a surprise to Kimball, because nearly a week into the trip he had forgotten exactly where they were heading next.

Trish Whitcomb gave up any idea of going to Poland at all because it was already clear that she wouldn't be able to get there in time for her talk. She persuaded Wayne Johnson to deliver their presentation by himself. She got VPN to change her flight so she could fly home from Bratislava.

A week earlier, no one would have just left the tour. A week later, common sense might have prevailed. After all, Andrew Frank had everything laid out for everyone. Here's your hotel, here's your room, here's your bus, here's your speaking venue, here's your microphone, here's your translator, here's a map for your free time, here's your food. Here's your Russian champagne.

Staying within the C&E bubble made being behind the Iron Curtain feel relatively safe. Leaving it was insane.

But on that particular day, following the heady evening in Juraj's apartment, it seemed not so much insane as inevitable. It was as if that evening had taken the visitors through some kind of looking glass into a different world.

They didn't speak the language. They didn't know anything about the country beyond what they'd learned in the space of about twenty-four hours. They didn't have a travel agent, mobile phones, or new technology. But they felt at home.

When VPN asked Trish Whitcomb, "Do you want to come to Bratislava?" she said, "I'll go get my bag." And walked out into the night.

The visitors were blown away by two things. One that the Slovaks wanted their help. And two that they felt they actually could help.

It turned out that when Kimball, Whitcomb, and Fadem had been improvising in Juraj's apartment about voter lists and polling, and different ways of setting up a campaign, they had been talking about things that VPN had never considered.

It was already apparent that there was a mismatch, however. The North Americans had the skills, but VPN didn't have the tools to carry out the job: no phone banks, no voter lists, and no party manifestos.

No one in the former communist bloc had that kind of stuff. They'd never needed it before.

CAMPAIGN OPTICS

Trish Whitcomb rode to Bratislava in the car with Juraj and Tanya, avoiding the discarded roof of the bus on the other carriageway. They talked about how society was changing and the influence of the Catholic Church, and about how Juraj's business had grown from a market stall to having a royalty deal with the government. They arrived in the evening, where Whitcomb spent more time speaking with other members of VPN before staying the night with a family. The next day she was back at the Mozart House talking to the party leaders.

They started by going over the North American visitors who had been in Juraj's apartment and reviewing their particular areas of expertise. The Slovakians were interested in who exactly might be able to help with what. They were also interested in raising money to help fund their campaign—they had very little financial backing—but Whitcomb had to disappoint them.

It wasn't simply a question of funneling funds from the United States to Slovakia. For one thing, US campaign finance rules forbade spending money on elections in other countries. For another, none of the C&E folk had the spare cash it would take to bankroll an election campaign.

Whitcomb told the VPN that Barry Fadem could guarantee an election victory if they allowed him to write their constitution. Then she thought she ought to clarify that she was kidding.

She had lunch with the VPN leader Ján Budaj and his translator. A media tour had been organized to draw attention to the Slovak election that would involve representatives from the VPN, the Christian Democrats, and the Greens touring Germany, the United States, and the Vatican. It was a way to increase international awareness of an election that tended to be overlooked compared with those happening in Prague and Budapest. Budaj was the VPN's chosen representative.

The original itinerary had the tour ending at the Vatican shortly before election day. That rang alarm bells for Whitcomb. She explained that images of a Christian Democrat with his arm around the Pope in Rome would not reflect well on the VPN in a largely Catholic country. Far better to rearrange the tour so that it ended in the United States, preferably with Budaj meeting US Vice President Dan Quayle.

Ján Budaj, the translator, and Whitcomb left the restaurant, walking the short distance to the offices of the Slovakian Parliament. Although she had no idea what the two men were saying, she figured that they were crafting a letter to the organizers of the three-country trip, and her guess proved right. After much dialogue, the translator read the letter in English. It delicately laid out a rationale for the change in routing without raising any suspicions that it would end in the United States—a political coup for VPN.

Later the North Americans learned that the other parties involved accepted the tour rerouting. In the event, Ján Budaj did not meet with Dan Quayle but with someone notable enough from the State Department to have made the trip worthwhile.

For Whitcomb, the optics of media coverage was 101 campaign stuff. For the Slovaks, it was completely new. They weren't used to media coverage of any kind. Whitcomb was struck by their lack of awareness of basics—voter contact, voter lists, door knocking, canvassing, going door to door—but kept reminding herself that this was a country that had never had a free election. The sort of campaign she was familiar with just didn't fit in a country that had really never had that kind of dialogue among the population about politics.

It was breathtaking. It made her think, "What have we gotten ourselves into?"

By the time she got to Bratislava airport for her flight back to the States, she was drained but elated. A few days earlier, the idea of walking into an airport alone in a country where she couldn't read the signs, let alone speak the language, would have been terrifying.

When her hosts said, "Do you want us to come in and help you?" she told them, "No, it's fine. I got this."

FLASHBACK

Barry Fadem watched as Trish Whitcomb drove off from Prague with a quick wave and a big smile. Almost immediately, he thought "What the hell am I doing?" Everyone else had gone, and suddenly he was alone in a city he barely knew with a handful of Slovaks who spoke little English. He thought about Kelly Kimball, who usually provided his support and backup, but was now headed with the others to Warsaw.

Perhaps, worried Fadem, he had bitten off more than he could chew. What on earth could he accomplish with the folks from VPN, or even contribute? It felt great to be involved—hell, it was really exciting—but he was painfully aware of two drawbacks. First, he wasn't a candidate campaign guy; he was an initiative campaign guy. So he might not be best placed to advise, anyway. And second, he only had thirty-six hours before he also needed to get to Warsaw ready for the end of the tour and the flight home.

Fadem recognized the members of VPN who first met him in Prague from the seminar the previous day in Bratislava, or from the evening at Juraj's apartment. He couldn't remember many names, but that didn't seem important. They seemed similar enough to be slightly interchangeable, and he would meet numerous other people over the next thirty-six hours who he was never introduced to, so he didn't know who they were or who they represented. All he knew was that they seemed to want to hear what he had to say: no meeting had fewer than six or eight people, and some up to more like twenty.

Fadem wasn't sure what knowledge he could add, but he had

been introduced at the seminar as an attorney who was a constitutional law expert, so as he was driven to the first meeting, he sat in the back of the car sketching out some notes he thought might be helpful. He divided the issues he thought he could talk about into two frames: winning the campaign first, and then governance issues second. They had to be raised together, really, because governance issues would inevitably be part of the campaign: whatever happened, it was clear that there was going to be a new constitution. That instantly raised questions: What rights would be specifically included for citizens? And what about the shape of the legislature itself? How long would elected representatives be in office? Would there be term limits?

As Fadem jotted down his notes and clarified his thoughts about the questions that needed to be answered, he was suddenly struck by a sense of excitement and intensity. "I'm in on the ground floor."

In this case, the ground floor turned out to be a room of about a dozen people. Fadem's first impression was of the cigarette smoke that was so thick in the air you could cut it with a knife. He tried not to cough. His second impression was the same feeling he had had the night before talking over beer and wine: "These are the people who made the revolution happen." They wanted to do their best for their country—and he wanted to help them.

Everyone was waiting for their guest to speak, and Fadem decided to use one of the techniques he and Kelly Kimball employed to get their audiences' attention: humor. "Ladies and gentlemen, in the United States we often talk about politicians meeting in smoke-filled rooms, like this one." He gestured generally to the air in the room. "When we do so, the idea is always negative. The idea is that whatever discussions take place in those rooms, whatever decisions are made, they are hidden from the public by the cloud of smoke. They are in the interests of the politicians, not of the people. They lack transparency. Ladies and gentlemen, where I come from, the smoke-filled room is a symbol of corruption.

"May I suggest that we throw every window in this room open to let every wisp of smoke escape and then start our discussion in the fresh air?"

To his amazement, a number of people jumped up and started opening windows while the other participants applauded.

Things were off to a good start.

Over the course of the next three hours and in subsequent meetings over the next day and a half, Fadem discussed every issue he could imagine that related to the preparation and adoption of a new constitution. He told his listeners, "Imagine you have a blank slate. You have complete freedom about what to include and what to leave out. Start by deciding your priorities for what is on either list."

That approach was enthusiastically embraced and the room filled with excited talk. It soon became clear, however, that the discussions were filled with a considerable amount of pent-up emotion from the years under communist rule. Someone asked Fadem, "How can you trust the government to conduct fair elections? Can you trust what government officials tell you about the results?"

Fadem struggled to find an answer. Usually, it would be enough simply to say, "Because that's how it works," but he realized how asinine that would likely sound in a roomful of people who all had very good reasons not to trust the government. These were the fears of people who were looking beyond the fact that they might actually form the next government to broader constitutional questions.

"When we talk about a constitution," they asked Fadem,

"that means endorsing the rule of law. But how can we guarantee that the judicial system will uphold the provisions of the constitution?"

No one said creating a constitution would be easy. Fadem had few simple answers because these were inherently profoundly difficult questions. Instead, he concentrated on discussing the American system of representative democracy. The bicameral model of the federal government through the Senate and the House was complicated for the Slovaks to understand, he could see. Hell, it was complicated enough for an American like him to understand, despite being a lawyer and despite having worked in politics his whole career—and it was not totally applicable to what their country faced.

Underlying every meeting and every discussion was the emotional issue of how people could trust the politicians they elected. Many of the participants were extremely suspicious of a new government controlling their lives.

"Why would we want to trade one very bad system for another bad system?" someone asked Fadem.

"What checks and balances can be built into the system to protect the people?" asked someone else.

Those would have been difficult questions even if everyone spoke the same language, thought Fadem. Someone always translated what he said into Czech, and enough of what others were saying for him to at least follow what was going on. It was frustrating, though. He could see that people were saying far more than was reaching his ears, and he desperately wanted to know what they were talking about. But waiting for translation was frustrating, even for him, as it constantly broke up the thread of the conversation. When emotions ran hot, no one bothered to wait. They all just addressed each other in Czech, speaking louder and louder.

Fadem watched them and wondered, "What are they arguing about this time?"

The meetings spent considerable time talking about the "power of the people." Fadem posed the questions that occurred to him in terms of the discussions he was familiar with about the United States Constitution. What rights would the people have, if any, to recall an elected official for any reason? What power, if any, should the people have with respect to voting on and rejecting government laws, in the form of referendums? What power, if any, should the people have to propose laws that the electorate would then get to vote on, in a similar way to how he and Kimball got initiatives onto the ballot in California?

Fadem could see the slight bemusement on people's faces as he put the questions and wondered if they were fair anyway. He clarified for his audience, "These are not really questions for today. These are questions for the long term. At the moment things like referendums and initiatives are a distraction from the main task, which is to introduce a democratic electoral system. I'm only raising these issues to provoke a discussion, as it were."

In that, Fadem could tell he was very successful. Loud and passionate conversations broke out throughout the room—almost entirely in Czech, which was always a sign that emotions were running high.

Having lit the fuse, Fadem could do nothing other than sit back and wait for the fire to burn itself out.

As far as he could see, the crux of the problem was very simple: who would the people trust? All of the participants in the meetings understood that a cornerstone of democracy was trust—trust in government, trust in their political party, and trust in their fellow citizens. After decades of not being able to trust much of everything, the country was desperate to be in a position to trust both government and themselves—and yet they found it inherently difficult to do so. They all realized, if they had not realized before, that the road to democracy would be difficult and potentially painful.

At the conclusion of his day and a half of meetings, Fadem was overcome with a variety of emotions as his new friends drove him to the airport to catch a flight to Warsaw to meet up with the C&E team before they all flew back to the United States. Most of all he was thankful. He was thankful to have been given the opportunity to have spent more time with some remarkably courageous individuals who had fought the battle to give their country true freedom. He was thankful for the opportunity to see people full of life as they began their journey down the very difficult road of democracy. For too many years, he reflected, the citizens of Czechoslovakia had virtually nothing to look forward to in their lives. The visitors had all been dazzled by the array of sweets available in the confectioners and bakeries of Bratislava and Prague—including pastry masterpieces, truffles of all sorts, and every type of dessert you could imagine—but that kind of indulgence was no substitute for true freedom.

As he boarded his plane for Warsaw, Fadem wished that the conversations of the previous thirty-six hours did not have to end, though he knew they did. He also knew that he would never forget the voices of the citizens he had met—voices infused with excitement and hope for a better future for everyone.

The whole experience was pretty mind-blowing for a state-based elections attorney from California.

When Fade got back home, he wondered what he had been thinking, trying to help write a constitution for a region that wasn't even a country. He was excited, but he was also aware that his excitement was largely based on speculation about what a constitution would look like and how it would be created and approved. But once back in the United States, Fadem realized *that he would need to be in the room while helping to write a constitution—and that was not going to be possible.*

CHAPTER 5

WARSAW

KELLY KIMBALL ARRIVED IN WARSAW WITH A HANGOVER and left with a commission to help the VPN win the federal elections in Slovakia. In between, he suffered some of the most anxious days of his life.

The problem was Barry Fadem. Kimball and Fadem were the Laurel and Hardy of California state ballot initiatives. One spoke, and the other reacted. The other spoke, with an equally comical response. Up and down the length of the Golden State.

It worked great in California. It worked great in Eastern Europe. When they hailed Budapest as the home of democracy in the new Europe, the Hungarians went nuts. When they explained in Prague that they hadn't been around for the American Revolution, so they didn't want to delay the Czech Revolution, the crowd went nuts again.

Now the minutes were ticking down to the presentation in Warsaw—and there was no Fadem.

To the best of Kimball's knowledge, Fadem was still in

Prague. When it was time to quit the Czech capital and move on, Fadem had said he would catch a later flight because of his meetings with VPN. To Kimball's mind, however, a later flight did not mean two days later. It didn't mean not showing up for a seminar.

Not only was there no sign of Fadem, but there was no way to find out anything about him or to get in touch with him. Kimball didn't know who Barry was with or even where he was. Trish Whitcomb had gone back to Bratislava with the VPN, so maybe Fadem had, too. But while Kimball felt confident that Whitcomb could look after herself, he was more anxious about his friend. Kimball simply wasn't used to being on trips without Fadem. In fact, he had rarely spoken in public without the other man. He felt very much alone.

Kimball kept asking everyone, has anybody heard from Barry? Has anyone seen him? Does anyone know where he's gone? No one knew. Of course, they didn't. If anyone was going to know, it would be Kimball.

Kimball and Fadem had history. Kimball had never given a speech to a group without Fadem sitting next to him so they could play off each other. He wasn't prepared for going solo. Up until five minutes before the speech, he kept thinking, "Maybe he's on his way from the airport right now" or "Barry's going to walk through the door." Even after he walked onto the stage and sat down at the table next to Fadem's chair. But the chair next to him stayed empty.

Even when Kimball started speaking, he still thought, "Any second, Barry's gonna come save me." But no.

Kimball might have pulled it off if the start of his talk wasn't sabotaged by a mishap that was not of his making. He opened by adapting the identical line Fadem had used about Prague in their presentation in Czechoslovakia, "Welcome to Warsaw, the cradle of democracy in Eastern Europe." In Prague, Fadem had been met with cheers of acclaim. But when Kimball said it in Warsaw, angry people in the audience took off their headphones and banged them on their desks.

It turned out that the interpreter had gotten confused about the use of the word "cradle" and her translation had come out as, "You guys are just babies." In other words, he'd just told the audience they were little more than infants.

There was no way back. Within minutes, Kimball realized that the whole speech was unsalvageable and thought, "Screw it. If they are going to be jerks, then so am I." Without his buddy to help out, he decided to grab his audience's attention by being a little more provocative. Facing a room of increasingly angry conservative Catholic Poles, he started to rile them up a little.

It was soon clear that he'd gone too far. Perhaps it was talking about legalizing marijuana. But it was probably telling them why abortion rights were a good thing. Twenty minutes into a two-hour speech, he simply stopped talking and walked off stage. The audience was howling mad. He had to get out of the room as quickly as possible—and then out of the building. And possibly out of the country.

The Canadian Greg Lyle had had a similarly frustrating time connecting with his Polish audience, though it wasn't Fadem related. He had even tried leaping off the stage to inject life into his presentation about managing the parliamentary side of politics and being in a minority administration. His ill-fated crowd surfing only ended with him getting hurt.

FLASHBACK

"Screw this," thought Kelly Kimball. When he met Greg Lyle, he

found the Canadian with an equally school's-out attitude that was echoed by another of his countrymen, Jerry Lampert. "Let's get out of here."

So they did. The three men left the ministry, hired a car, and set out across the Polish countryside. Destination: the notorious death camps at Auschwitz–Birkenau. As they left the disappointments of Warsaw behind them, the three men relaxed, but there was little chatter. It probably reflected the somber quality of their destination.

At Auschwitz, the three men paid their entrance fee and walked in through the infamous gates with the motto, Arbeit Macht Frei—"Work makes you free"—and spent four hours exploring the vast site, seeing the barbed wire, the rail station, and the barracks. For Kimball, the experience couldn't quite be described as enlightening, given that everyone already knew what had happened in the camps. Instead, it was simply emotionally draining.

From Auschwitz, they made their way to the death camp at Birkenau, next door. When they got there, thick fog made it impossible to see anything as they climbed to the viewpoint on a wall overlooking the site. Then the fog slowly started lifting. First, they began to make out the few barracks buildings that remained and the tracks that carried the crowded rail wagons packed with Jews from across Europe. And then it revealed the chimneys that loomed over the site like headstones. It gave the whole place the impression of being like a vast graveyard—which, in many ways, it was.

That evening, Kimball, Lyle, and Lampert drove into Krakow for dinner. They ate in a marvelous restaurant that was 700 years old, frozen in a period of elegance and grace. The contrast between the refinement and the barbarism they had seen that afternoon was profound and deeply depressing.

Kimball told the others, "That was one of the worst, most horrible, and most amazing experiences of my life." Compared with Auschwitz, any other memorial to the Holocaust he had ever seen seemed like sad Disneyland versions of the grim reality.

Kimball reflected deeply on the visit, and it would have life-changing effects for him and his family. He was an Irish Catholic—indeed, his brother had become a priest—but his wife was the only daughter of a Jewish family. The recent birth of their son, who was little more than a month old, had prompted them to reflect on in which religion to raise their kids. The visit to the camps removed any doubt from Kimball's mind. Face to face with the brutal apparatus the Nazis had put in place to try to exterminate the Jews, it suddenly seemed vital to him that his son be raised Jewish to continue his family line.

WOMEN AND OTHER QUESTIONS

The venerable restaurant in Krakow was one of the more refined experiences the C&E party had in Poland. Warsaw itself felt unwelcoming and seedy. There was a highly visible sex trade. Andrew Frank and a colleague spent an awkward evening in the hotel bar where the only other guests were call girls who obviously saw the American men as their potential customers for the night.

The C&E seminar was held in an official ministry building where everyone felt that they were being watched—and they probably were. Frank had only selected it because it already had translation booths in place.

At one point during the seminar, some of the Poles began discussing the role of women in politics. Some became visibly upset at the very idea. "Why," they kept asking, "would women be in politics? What could they contribute?" They directed the questions to female advisors who had made a career in politics. One man asked, "How, if women were in government, it would be possible to avoid a war every twenty-eight days?"

The Americans didn't know what to make of a debate in those terms.

In Hungary, where women were equally new to politics, there had also been questions about their involvement. But even there, women didn't have to prove that they were capable of being involved at all. Women who had attended the seminar in Budapest had asked Trish Whitcomb what they should wear. She told them to look business-like but that dressing like a man was not necessary to be effective.

But in Poland, it wasn't women's clothes that were under scrutiny. It was their very ability to be involved in politics at all. It was like going back to the days before the Nineteenth Amendment.

Women were just one of the groups facing a jaw-dropping amount of prejudice. There was constant antisemitism. One popular female talk-radio host, the Rush Limbaugh of Poland, repeated over and over the message that Jews were destroying the economy and were responsible for all the unemployment in the country.

Another common target was the Roma. Many people at the seminar didn't want the Roma to be included. Kimball tried to explain that they had to let everyone take part in the seminar, but the Poles explained, "You nice people from America don't understand that these people are terrible. They can't be here. They will ruin what you're doing. You're naïve, kind, and generous, but let us explain why the Roma cannot possibly be here."

What soon became apparent was that their attitude had little to do with the Roma, specifically. The prevailing attitude was that the Poles had been screwed for the last forty years, so now they were going to do it to somebody else. Now it was the Poles' turn to screw with someone, so they chose the Roma.

The consultants had been aware of a similar attitude wherever they went. It was the unenlightened underbelly of democracy. It was an important principle of democracy that C&E didn't censor their audiences. Anybody who wanted to come was free to attend the sessions. That was the whole point. But that came with lots of dangers. There were plenty of former communists who were still around, former fascists, and lots of people who were crazy in one way or another. As the one-party state collapsed, many peripheral parties emerged that were not entirely attractive from a Western liberal point of view—or even just from a sane point of view.

That was part of the risk. Setting up the seminars was like a metaphor for democracy itself. C&E drummed up customers and hoped the events weren't taken over by the crazies.

It was a salutary reminder of how fragile the foundations of democracy can be.

BARBERSHOP DUET

If Czechoslovakia was still enjoying the drunkenness of the revolution, Poland was suffering from the hangover.

For nearly a decade, Poland had been the poster child for democracy in Eastern Europe. Solidarnosc, the Solidarity trade union, had emerged from the shipyards of Gdansk to challenge the communist rule. Led by Lech Walesa, who had become the figurehead of the rebellion, the union led mass strikes and street demonstrations through the spring and summer of 1988 until they forced the authorities to agree to elections.

Walesa was a star. Like Václav Havel. They were the John Lennon and Paul McCartney of revolution.

Like everyone else, the C&E group had been excited to get to Poland. They were enamored of Lech Walesa and Solidarity. Kelly Kimball and his new Republican buddy, Wayne Johnson, were determined to get hold of some Solidarity ephemera. Everywhere they had been, the visitors had collected bumper stickers, posters, buttons: anything they could get their hands on. The material was better designed, more striking, more humorous, and covetable—and more historical—than campaign ephemera in the United States. Everyone came home from the trip weighed down with souvenirs.

Kimball and Johnson set out together to find the Solidarity headquarters. The young leftist and the religiously conservative Republican climbed into a cab and tried, in their best Polish, to get the driver to understand where they wanted to go. "Solidarnosch," they told him. They probably even pronounced it properly, given that it had been on every US TV and radio news bulletin for many years.

When the message finally got through, the driver tripped the meter and started driving. But instead of heading into Warsaw, he drove them out of town. The Americans had assumed that such a big-deal party would have its HQ closer to the center.

They drove through nondescript outskirts for thirty minutes, then forty-five minutes, before the driver finally dropped them off on what seemed to be an abandoned street and pointed them to an alley. It was like a scene from a John le Carré novel where an intelligence agent is being set up. But, like idiots, they went down the alley as instructed.

Only to find themselves facing the Solidarnosc Hair Salon. Which was, in any case, closed.

It was the end of the day, and that neighborhood had emptied out, including the cab driver counting his tip as he wondered why two American tourists with a lime-green surf bag had chosen to have their hair cut at this particular salon.

The two Americans stood on the street corner for an hour, trying to figure out how to get the hell out of there. There was no sign of a bus stop and not many cars. They saw a few cabs but were unable to flag one down.

They got more frustrated—and desperate—until Johnson had an epiphany. He decided that the reason they couldn't get a ride was because of Kimball's bag. He announced that a lime-green bag would make people assume that they were gay. Which, in a country still emerging from the dead hand of communist orthodoxy, was hardly likely to endear them to any potential rides.

Apart from rejecting Johnson's interpretation of fashion semiotics, for Kelly Kimball, the moment was a snapshot of a key dynamic of the entire trip. One of the reasons he had gone to Eastern Europe in the first place was to meet other US political consultants and gain more insight into the profession. It was a chance to see if he could get on with people from different ends of the political spectrum with whom he didn't normally get a chance to interact.

When you're on the other side of a campaign, you instinctively begin not to like the players on the opponent's team. And from experience, often, you learn not to trust them. It was an eye-opener to realize that you could. Not that it should have come as a surprise. Consultants on both sides tend to be drawn to politics by the process rather than the policies or beliefs. No wonder they're all similar.

At the time, it seemed to the people from C&E that there were as many political consultants in Poland as there were at home. People from all over North America and Europe were heading to Warsaw, and even to Gdansk, to talk about democracy or elections. Everyone was eager to give the Poles the benefit of their advice. The result was an absolute glut of political information of varying quality from sources ranging from the authoritative to the chancer. And none of the political noise was filtered.

It was already getting more difficult to change things, however. The political process in Poland had already hardened into shape. Lots of people had already been there, and the system was established. There were gatekeepers, there were bureaucrats, and there were elites. And there were the excluded, the supplicants, the masses.

In Poland, they were nothing more than political consultants with little to contribute—or at least, little that people wanted to listen to. It was another contrast with Bratislava, where they had been able to sit down with the revolutionaries themselves. The people who caused the trouble in what would become the Slovakian Republic were left to their own devices. Like Prague, Warsaw underlined to the visitors how lucky they had gotten to be in the right place at the right time.

DISSOLVING COMMUNISM

As a preacher, Dr. James Noble was naturally concerned with the future of Christianity in a democratic Eastern Europe. Under communism, courses in atheism had been mandatory in schools, but educators were not permitted to teach the Christian religion to children. Nevertheless, the region had an underlying deeply conservative Catholicism (John Paul II, who became pope in 1978, was a Pole).

At Noble's workshop in Prague, two young college students

told him that they were interested in learning about the faith but that they didn't know anything about the Bible or Jesus. They asked him, "How can we find out about that?"

Such a basic question left him dumbfounded.

On arriving in Warsaw, Noble was struck by seeing all the scaffolding erected while workers removed flags, signs, and name boards. To see the physical trappings of communism being taken away came as a stark reminder of the fragility of any kind of political system—including democracy. No matter how strong its physical appearance is, a system can collapse as easily as its symbols.

There was no better metaphor for the collapse of the communist system than the fact that some 1,800 buildings in Warsaw associated with the former regime were up for sale.

Andrew Frank would notice the same in Bratislava when he thought about buying a former police station to turn into a bar. He planned to name it Rok Rok, as "rok" is Slovak for year, Rock Year. A great name for a bar. And a name that remains unused, the cost of the abandoned building equating to half a million US dollars.

That's a lot of $25 daily stipends.

FLASHBACK

Where was Barry?

Kelly Kimball had had a tough couple of days in Poland. The solo seminar had gone badly. His visit to Auschwitz and Birkenau had been emotionally devastating.

And Barry was still missing.

Kimball was no longer worried about his speech. That had been and gone. The damage was done—and it was lasting. But Kimball's performance anxiety had been replaced by a rising sense of dread. What if something had happened to Barry? Something serious? What if there had been some comeback from the authorities about the broken bus? What if people in the government had taken a dim view of Barry's meeting with the VPN?

As he lay on the bed in his hotel room, Kimball's mind raced through a range of possibilities from the highly likely to the frankly impossible. They all shared one thing: none of them ended well for Barry Fadem.

Kimball was a huge fan of Hunter S. Thompson, which made things worse. His imagination kept putting together images of people who were subversive and out of control with images from other sources of Communist methods of control, repression, and punishment.

"What's happened to Barry?" Kimball had no idea. As time went on, however, he became more convinced that something had happened to his friend. He checked the hotel phone to see if he could figure out how he could start ringing prisons in Prague— then stopped when he realized that he didn't even know what prisons there were in Prague. Or police stations. Or hospitals.

He had no information and no obvious way of getting any, and that lack of knowledge only made him feel more helpless. He'd grown quite accustomed to Eastern Europe over the past couple of weeks—but now it suddenly seemed a very alien and unsettling place again.

In his head, he was already making the phone call to Fadem's wife to tell her that Barry was missing somewhere in Eastern Europe. And she was already asking him, "Why did you leave him there on his own?"

That was the question echoing in Kimball's head. "Why did I leave him?" Though, to be honest, his guilt was more to do with his own paranoia about being parted from the man who was his constant companion on political tours and speaking engagements than it was to do with Barry's ability to look after himself.

He looked at his watch. The time was getting closer to head for the airport to fly back to the States. In the back of his mind, Kimball was already starting to think of the decision he would have to make. Would he leave Barry behind?

He wondered if there was any way to get in touch with the VPN in Prague. What had they wanted with Barry anyway? Kimball had assumed that the lawyer would have a short meeting with them to discuss constitutional matters, but what if they hadn't been satisfied? What if they had somehow taken Barry back to Bratislava with them? What if he had been taken against his will?

"I should never have left him," thought Kimball, miserably. With hindsight, that was obvious. This was all his own fault, not Barry's. That's how Barry's wife would see it, too. She might not say it, but she would be thinking it. Kimball dreaded calling her to tell her the news, but it seemed increasingly inevitable that he would have to. "I don't know where Barry is, I don't know what he's doing, and I don't know how he'll be getting home. Or when."

Kimball was growing more and more worried and more and more convinced that something had happened to Barry. He started to wonder whether Andrew Frank would have contacts who would be able to help ring around the hospitals, police stations, and prisons in Prague to try to locate his friend.

It was the last evening of the tour, and all the fellow travelers were ready to celebrate their new-found friendships. Not Kimball. He lay on his bed feeling sick with nerves about Barry, and wracked with guilt that his friend was somewhere in the middle of Eastern Europe, isolated and probably in big trouble.

There was a bang on the door. Kimball assumed it was someone inviting him for a drink or wanting to exchange phone *numbers. But when he opened the door, there was Barry Fadem, none the worse for wear.*

Fadem walked into the room and said, "We're running an election."

Kimball looked at his friend with relief. He wasn't sure whether to shout at him, hit him, or hug him. Like a parent when a young teenager comes in at 3:00 a.m., he didn't know whether to be mad or relieved. So he just said, "OK. How much are we making?"

Fadem replied, "Nothing, but we've got a contract."

Kimball asked, "So why are we doing it?"

"Because it's going to be fun." Though on reflection, he probably included some more colorful swearing to underline his excitement.

At that moment, Kimball was too relieved to object to the plan. Not that he had any intention of doing so. He didn't have a choice. The deal was done. The contract wasn't just a figure of speech—it was a signed piece of paper in Barry's hand.

A SENSE OF MISSION

And it *would* be fun. And different. And interesting. And, like the others, Kimball had found the people from VPN inspiring. As the two reunited friends discussed the project later in the hotel bar, he realized how much he wanted to help.

They all wanted to help. The people they had met in Bratislava had been remarkable. They were prepared to be arrested to claim their democratic rights. They *had* been arrested.

The young Americans were thrilled because they could see a way they *could* help. By the time they were all back in the United States, and Andrew Frank was headed back to the

UK, they had a plan. Trish Whitcomb was already a yes. In short order, Andrew Frank was a yes, because he had become fascinated by the situation in Eastern Europe. And because he didn't really have anything else lined up.

Fadem and Kimball had identified Frank as the ideal man to be on the ground while the others raised money in the United States. Because whatever came next, it was going to cost money. Kimball, Fadem, and Whitcomb, along with Greg Lyle and Ginny Kotnick, formed a non-profit that they named *Volunteers for Democracy.* It turned out to be largely funded by the founders, but nonetheless, raised a decent budget.

Even if it was only enough for Andrew Frank to buy ice cream in Bratislava.

CHAPTER 6

BACK TO BRATISLAVA

ANDREW FRANK ARRIVED BACK IN LONDON WITH A BRICK he'd kicked out of the Berlin Wall, only to find that his flight attendant friend was clearly not such a friend any longer, because he found all his belongings outside her apartment.

Frank had driven back from Warsaw with an American friend via Berlin and Amsterdam. They had arrived in Berlin the night of election night in March of 1990. It was the first free elections in Eastern Germany. They crossed the border back and forth at Checkpoint Charlie three or four times, just for fun, including once with a couple of girls they had met in east Berlin. The Americans drove their new friends into West Berlin, although the girls had actually already been there once the wall had unofficially opened some months earlier. The East German border guards at Checkpoint Charlie didn't understand what was going on as they watched the car go back and forth—which only increased the fun.

There were fireworks on the East Berlin side, and Frank

took his brick out of the wall. It would end up in a clear plexiglass box on his desk, with lots of banknotes from different places he had since visited around the world.

Frank felt that he was at the tail end of history. The wall had come down months earlier, but that event had been the trigger point of why he had wanted to visit Europe in the first place. It seemed highly appropriate to get to Berlin just in time for the elections, which in the eyes of many observers had become an important symbol of freedom.

The trip also shaped Frank's future. He became a young leader with the American Council on Germany, a relationship he has maintained for decades. When he later worked for President Clinton, he went to Vienna as a spokesperson for the human rights conference. All that had been kicked off by seeing the twin newspaper headlines: "Florio Wins Big" and "Berlin Wall Falls."

That was when he decided that he didn't want to stay in New Jersey government and headed to Eastern Europe instead.

From Berlin, Frank headed to Amsterdam and then to London. Within a few days, he was back in Bratislava. That wasn't just because of his frosty reception in London. It was also because he had been in touch with the C&E folks, who told him, "Let's do this."

So Frank went back to Bratislava while the others were setting up Volunteers for Democracy as a 501 C3 nonprofit. Barry Fadem had already spoken to him about the possibility of going back, and Frank reasoned that he had no plans in the United States. Nor, it was now clear, in London. So he agreed to be the man on the ground with VPN. It was a gamble based on an acquaintance of little over a week, but it was obvious to everyone that Frank was a safe pair of hands.

Plus, he remained very cheap.

After his $25 dollars a day from C&E, he went back to Slovakia earning not much more from his former charges, who were now his new employers.

Luckily for Frank, the VPN found him an apartment belonging to a television producer who became the party's ad man, Anton Mrazek, and his wife Iveta. They lived downstairs and, with their two young daughters, treated Frank like a member of the family. The younger daughter, Vanda, a cute five-year-old, took a curious liking to the young visitor who didn't speak her language. He also got along well with the older teenage daughter, Ruthie, and was later able to sponsor her to visit the United States for a year of high school in New Jersey. Without them, Juraj Mihalik, his wife Tanya, and the friendly nature of many VPN people, the experience in Bratislava would have been very different.

The Mrazeks lived on the top of the wooded hill above the downtown area, which was the toney end of Bratislava. Frank's neighbors there included Alexander Dubček, who led Czechoslovakia during the Prague Spring in 1968, and was probably the most famous living Slovak.

Every day, Frank walked down the hill to the VPN headquarters in the Mozart House and often stopped to eat ice cream. On his way back up the hill, he stopped for a delicious local beer.

The agreement with Volunteers for Democracy was that Andrew Frank would stay in Bratislava for the time until the election to advise VPN. To say that he was out of his depth was an understatement. He was winging it and seeking advice from his colleagues in the United States about how best to be helpful.

As far as VPN were concerned, it was clear that Frank was

useful simply by being there. He was the only American consistently in Bratislava at a time when many people there felt an affinity with the United States and wanted to learn as much about it as possible. They wanted to understand its political system. They listened to Radio Free Europe and Voice of America to find out more about US attitudes toward the world—and to learn English. Everyone seemed convinced that their future would be English-speaking. When some French educators arrived with a plan to set up a French academy, they were thwarted by the fact that the Slovaks were far more interested in learning English than French.

Everyone welcomed Frank, and for the next three months, he became part of a very intense period of their lives. He also, however, found time for some more personal projects, including visiting the town of Sered with his father, who had come over to Vienna for a business trip. They explored the town where his great-grandfather had emigrated to the United States in 1908.

Wind of what Frank and Volunteers for Democracy were doing eventually got out, though it didn't raise a huge amount of interest. The men's magazine *Details* sent a reporter to Bratislava. She spent ten days there with Frank and a friend she'd brought along, together with a Canadian photographer who turned up for a day and a half around the actual election, which he spent taking photos but mostly getting drunk.

Frank insisted that the reporter had complete access to the party's operations. It was normal in the United States, but it upset many of his new colleagues. In the former Soviet states, having someone follow you around with a notebook was something that never ended well. And in the end, the story came to nothing, which upset Frank. The journalist wrote her piece—she sent Frank a copy—but someone at *Details* came to their senses about just how interested fashion-conscious young American males were in Slovakia.

The article was quietly dropped.

VOLUNTEERS FOR DEMOCRACY

As soon as they got home from Eastern Europe, Trish Whitcomb, Kelly Kimball, Greg Lyle, Ginny Kotnik, and Barry Fadem started setting up an organization to try to win an election in a country they had barely known existed only a few weeks earlier.

Strictly speaking, it wasn't a country, only a republic of the Czechoslovak federation.

They did the paperwork to set up a bona fide 501(c)(3) corporation, Volunteers for Democracy. The title was ambitious, but as a money-raising operation, it left a lot to be desired. In fact, it was almost entirely funded by the handful of people involved. There was no time to organize anything else, with the elections just a couple of months away.

The travelers who had been in Bratislava were excited, but the people they asked for money were far less so. No one wanted to fund some obscure political operators to work in an obscure part of Europe. So the time came when they looked at each other and said, "Well, we'd better keep putting money into this thing ourselves."

They kept writing checks—because there wouldn't be any other checks.

Being in the right place at the right time had proven quite expensive.

DEMOCRACY IS MESSY

One of Frank's messages to the Slovaks was that democracy is always messy.

VPN were already starting to figure that out for themselves. The young dissident Martin Šimečka had been part of the revolution but, in its aftermath, soon realized that society couldn't simply be left in the hopes that democracy would inevitably emerge. He and his companions had already noticed that the Christian Democrats had started to work to establish themselves as a political party. They had assistance from their fellow Christian Democrats in Germany. VPN, on the other hand, was finding it difficult to crystallize into a party suitable to fight an election.

That made VPN realize that they could not simply leave the revolution to itself. They had to take responsibility for whatever came next, and they had to do that by changing themselves into a political movement.

The people behind the revolution were too broad to form a single political party with shared policies and aims. Instead, they had the idea of forming a political movement, VPN, that would be outside the usual structures of party politics.

Frank noted with interest the problems that came along with that commitment to inclusiveness. As a vessel for anyone who was against the communist regime and wanted change, VPN included groups with a broad range of views. Some were social liberals; others were more nationalistic. Although Slovakia was clearly then part of Czechoslovakia, clear nationalistic tendencies were growing that would eventually contribute to its becoming independent. At the time, however, it was only a direction of travel, and the VPN leadership didn't really try to distance the movement from the nationalists. That would come to prove a fateful development.

Meanwhile, other people who were close to Havel were going to go to the national government, whereas others were going to stay in the Slovak government. The politician who became the federal cultural minister in Havel's government in Prague had a very different view of things than somebody who stayed around to fight for something in Slovakia.

VPN was a diverse group of people who were clearly against something and who shared a cause. They were all genuinely interested in achieving change and trying to do good things for the people. During the run-in to the election, however, while Frank was with them, they were starting to figure out what they were *for*—and that was when they realized that they were not all in sync. Ultimately, the tensions that were already present led to the fragmentation and rejiggering of political parties after the elections, when the broad-based movement lost its luster, and better-defined parties took its place.

At the time, the country was being run by an interim federal government. To the disappointment of many Slovaks, however, it was not making many efforts to begin a process of change. It didn't even include the people who had led the revolution. Instead, it was largely made up of former communists—or even people who were still communists. By the time elections came in June 1990, many Slovaks were tired of waiting for a process of change to begin.

FALLING CHANCES

Fedor Gál and Martin Bútora, two senior figures in the VPN, were friends and psychologists who pioneered opinion polling in Slovakia (the agency they founded remains the leading agency in the country). The two men introduced Western polling techniques that allowed VPN to become the first group in the country to get an insight into how their fellow citizens thought and how they had reacted to the revolution.

The figures were devastating. The popularity of the VPN had fallen steeply, with its approval rate tanking from about 40 percent to just 10 percent in a couple of months. Other parties were growing more popular, including not just the Christian Democrats but also new bodies, such as the Slovak National Party, who were nationalists, and the Party of the Democratic left formed by former communists, who were recasting themselves as some kind of social democrats.

A number of these new parties had become more popular than the movement that actually started the revolution.

It made the former revolutionaries feel a little underappreciated. It also made them feel responsible. Some of the undercurrents unleashed in Slovak politics by the fall of Communism were potentially harmful—not least the former communists themselves in their barely believable new guise. Their commitment to both society and democracy was highly questionable. The Christian Democrats meanwhile had a toxic history, because in World War II Slovakia, then a separate state, had been ruled as a fascist republic with the cooperation of the Catholic hierarchy. When the Christian Democrats began to campaign for the region to go back to its roots, that rang alarm bells. Slovak nationalists clearly threatened the very existence of Czechoslovakia with their calls for Slovak independence.

Meanwhile, ordinary Slovaks found themselves, for the first time, having to choose people to represent them. This meant that they had to think about who they really were, and whether they saw themselves as Christian Democrats, because they were Catholic, or social democrats because they distrusted capitalism. It was a new way to think about themselves that most people weren't used to.

Šimečka and his colleagues concluded that VPN could not simply abandon the stage. They needed to take responsibility for the forces they had helped to unleash. In their own view, they had to become the saviors of both democracy in the face of a possible reaction from the former communists, but also of the whole Czechoslovak Federation in the face of the growing voices of nationalism.

They had no choice but to try to win the election, even though to begin with it had not intended to even take part, having achieved its purpose simply by bringing down the Soviet-backed government. And the result wasn't a foregone conclusion. Slovakia wasn't like the rest of Czechoslovakia, where Civic Forum would clearly stroll to victory.

VPN would have to fight.

SUPPING WITH THE DEVIL

Martin Šimečka's father, Milan, was one of the most senior dissidents and a sophisticated political thinker. He argued that VPN had to win the elections, and in order to do that they needed popular candidates. And that involved making compromises with former communists. He picked three men whose popularity suggested they should be near the top of the candidate list. Alexander Dubček, the chairman of the federal parliament and prime minister of the Soviet government, was the hero of the Prague Spring; Milan Čič, the minister of justice in the communist government, promoted himself as a new Democrat and was popular mainly because he didn't seem to do much and came across as a reasonably decent guy, even though he was still widely seen as a crook.

The Slovak minister of the interior, Vladimír Mečiar, was another popular figure.

VPN's best campaigners included Ján Budaj and Milan Kňažko, who had a following as a former actor. They were dynamic speakers who generated big crowds at rallies and meetings throughout Slovakia. But Šimečka Sr argued that even such outstanding performers lagged far behind the former communists in popularity. Working with the former enemy represented VPN's best chance of winning the election.

It is a truism of post-revolutionary politics that not all activists become good politicians—just as not all politicians are good activists. To make the shift, someone needs to be a good speaker who is persuasive and willing to take risks. Because of that, the early leaders of VPN, much like the early leaders in other countries, were young, aspirational, and had some charisma. Leaders elsewhere, such as Lech Walesa and Václav Havel, had more of a moral authority that they were bringing to the table. But the VPN leaders all had something that they were bringing to the table. Others found it far more difficult to turn their activism and anti-communist rhetoric into action.

It was ironic that Volunteers for Democracy had ended up fighting to get a bunch of former communists into power, even if the communists had switched sides. That was part of Andrew Frank's contribution to the debate in Bratislava. He introduced VPN to the basic rules of campaigns and elections. And the most basic one of all was that the campaign alone was not enough. If you couldn't win elections, you had nothing. And to win elections, you have to make deals and compromises. Even with your former enemies.

POLITICS 101

VPN faced a situation in which few people knew much about what they were doing—and what would happen. The polling being carried out by Fedor Gál and his associates was far more philosophical and esoteric in terms of the questions it asked than Western pollsters would ask. It wasn't just, *Who do you want to vote for? What are your top three issues? Does this message resonate?* Gál's polling went far deeper into people's self-identification, although many people were still reluctant to talk to pollsters, given the hangover from the authoritarian past.

For a twenty-five-year-old with limited experience in US politics, Gál was a figure of great respect whose polling was helping VPN figure out what they wanted to do and how they were going about it. Gál later created the Institute for Polling, which was very successful. His work taught Frank that having a bigger picture can be necessary to understand the little things. Gál and the others felt they needed to understand the bigger picture in order to drill down even more.

It was very different from received US wisdom about polling and media analysis, but Frank acknowledged that it suited the political landscape, which was completely different from the situation in the United States. In some parts of Slovakia, older people who had been living under communism for so long—and who had survived World War II—had more of an affinity towards the old system because it provided just enough for them to live. For them, that was enough. Younger people, however, and people who became more educated—whether they educated themselves or were lucky enough to go to certain universities—were able to see a bigger picture of a changing Europe and changing strategic alliances.

The map of Slovakia stretches from Bratislava in the west

to Nitra, then Banská Bystrica in the center of the county, and Košice and Prešov toward the border with Ukraine in the east. These cities are far from the capital, lying in the mountains of central Slovakia and the rich farmland in the east. Far from Bratislava, where the country is more rural and less industrial, people tended to be less inclined to be supportive of big change and more confused. Confusion was one of the main emotions everywhere, along with uncertainty, particularly among ordinary Slovaks who were mainly interested in keeping their jobs or having a way to make money to feed their families.

VPN spent a lot of time discussing how to educate people in rural areas. It wasn't just a question of getting their support for VPN but getting them to understand that democracy in itself was a good thing for them. They had to convince people who did not really understand the importance or benefits of elections that they should turn out and vote.

VPN was the driving force for education throughout the country, along with Civic Forum in the Czech Republic. They were the driving force on television and on the ground to educate people about the elections. Frank and the others helped create the tools that educated people that they should vote, that they should participate in a democratic process, and that they needed to understand what they were against and what they were for because they had a chance to shape their own futures.

The process was inherently more esoteric than in the United States because there were none of the fixed points or tramlines of an established democratic political system. The whole debate took place on a broader level.

It also took place in an atmosphere lacking in trust. It was impossible for pollsters simply to ask people who they were going to vote for, or what policies they supported. The answer was likely to be, "Why should I tell you? Are you the secret police?" There were secret police still around throughout Eastern Europe because the police and security apparatus couldn't simply be dismantled the day after the communist governments fell. There was a movement to weed out secret police and informers, but Havel had called for this to be done with "a human face." In other words, the secret police were being exposed, but they weren't being purged or killed.

As part of the process of educating voters, Kimball and Fadem came up with the idea of distributing a draft ballot to show people what they would see when they walked into the polling booth. It was common in California and elsewhere to receive a sample ballot in the mail so that voters on election day had half a clue about what they were looking at.

Their idea was based on the fact that ballots in places like California were often insanely complicated. Some of that insanity was partly because of the efforts of initiative specialists like Fadem and Kimball to add various propositions to the ballot paper. Now their knowledge was put to use to clarify what voters would see.

VPN liked that idea.

They also published a series of small cards to hand out with caricatures of their politicians. They were kind caricatures, and the whole atmosphere was relaxed. There were hundreds of thousands, to make people familiar with the politicians. They helped get the voters excited during the campaign. People loved having something to collect.

It was a far cry from the Hungarians and their miniature screeds of tiny bullet points.

In general, Andrew Frank found it difficult to convince his colleagues to concentrate on the practicalities. They were a talking shop. Day after day, the Mozart House was home to large meetings of twenty or more people sitting around sharing their opinions and holding debates.

One time, they were talking about posters. Posters played a vital role in politics in the region as part of the Soviet and Eastern European tradition of using striking visual art to appeal to voters who did not have access to TVs or newspapers, or who were not highly literate. The VPN leadership had its own graphics team, and its own printing operation and the selected designs were printed in their thousands. They were piled up downstairs in the basement ready to be distributed throughout the country and pasted to the walls.

The posters were designed to be as memorable and direct as possible. One of the favorites showed a rainbow with the slogan "Good morning Slovakia."

To Frank's dismay, the VPN leaders started going over the choice of posters again. It was typical of their tendency to fall back into their habits as an underground caucus debating ideas like philosophy professors. Frank kept telling them they could not run a campaign by consensus.

The conversation went around in a circle and everyone was starting to disagree. Does this poster make sense or not?

This was typical of life under communism when the dissidents had nothing to do except debate. They were far more comfortable debating topics than making decisions. Under communism, there was rarely any need to decide anything.

The regime decided everything for you.

In this meeting, after much debate and bickering, the translator stopped translating. The argument went on for another ten minutes. Then Frank stood up and shocked everyone: "Guys, we agreed to all the slogans for the posters last week. We already decided what the messages were. Let's just get them out and distribute them."

Juraj pointed at Frank and said, "I knew you were CIA. I always knew you were CIA." Then the room cracked up.

It was one of the few moments of light relief during an intense period.

Then they distributed the posters as planned.

EARLY SPLITS

When it came time for the VPN to select a leader for the party they ended up with Ján Budaj.

It turned out it was like booking a ticket on the *Titanic*.

There were already splits within VPN that would lead to seismic changes and eventually to the division of Czechoslovakia into the Czech and Slovakian Republics. Budaj and Milan Kňažko had become more nationalistic than many of their colleagues. They were eager to stress their Slovak heritage at any opportunity, unlike their colleagues who believed that the survival of Czechoslovakia as one country was paramount.

The program of VPN itself was consciously non-nationalistic. It concentrated entirely on democratic values. But everyone knew it was a compromise, given the presence of a strong nationalistic tendency within the movement.

One of the problems was that most VPN leaders didn't want to run in elections. Most of them didn't want to be politicians or stand for election. That allowed the most popular leaders of the movement to become even more visible.

Looking back, it was a fateful decision.

THE BALL GAME

Frank's status as the only American in Bratislava was cemented when the Harlem Globetrotters turned up as part of a tour of Eastern Europe to celebrate the fall of communism.

Frank had carried his sneakers back and forth across Europe in the hope that he would be able to shoot some hoops in different countries. They had rarely come out of his bag. Basketball was still pretty new in the Eastern bloc. He also wasn't very good, so he welcomed the chance to enjoy the game as a spectator.

One of the VPN leaders got Frank a ticket right behind the Globetrotters' bench. During the game, he said to no one in particular, "You guys are awesome."

One of the players turned around and said "You speak English?"

"Yeah, I'm from New Jersey."

"What do you mean, you're from New Jersey? Where are we? Why are you here?"

Frank told him why.

"Where are you from in New Jersey?"

"North Brunswick."

The Globetrotters had a player from Bayonne, so the player tells him, "Hey, this guy's from New Jersey. This guy's from Jersey."

The whole team made a fuss of Frank for the rest of the game, which was fun in a 10,000-seat arena.

The Globetrotters weren't the only people who were curious about what Frank was doing in Bratislava. He wasn't part of big groups like the National Democratic Institute or the International Republican Institute. He was part of a private group that had arrived with *Campaigns & Elections* and then stayed around to help run the campaign. Frank got called to the embassy in Prague by the then-political officer to explain why he was there and what he was doing. Andrei Bartosevicz drove him to Prague.

Presumably, Frank's answers were acceptable. At any rate, he was allowed to continue his role without further interference.

NEW TECHNOLOGY

In the United States Kelly Kimball was trying to send some computers to the VPN headquarters.

It had taken a week to get the computers to the Slovakian border with Austria, and another month to get them across. The customs officials expected a bribe to release them, and VPN didn't have enough money to pay it.

No one could get the computers released. It was frustrating to pay for things that weren't going to arrive in a timely fashion. And that had no earthly use if they arrived late.

At the time, before the Internet, most computers were being used to make spreadsheets and play Lemmings. But VPN had identified a lack of computers as one of their problems and believed it would help the campaign if they could distribute them around the country.

Kimball marked them for the attention of the VPN's IT specialist, a large doughy guy, who finally received them after Kimball took it upon himself to find out who he needed to wire money to pay the bribe.

As a token of gratitude, he received a book of Václav Havel's plays, signed by the author.

PROFESSIONAL PROGRAM

Andrew Frank told the VPN, "This campaign needs to be a professional thing. You can't do it like dissidents and volunteers."

The Christian Democrats and communists had international support and money. Especially the Christian Democrats. VPN had money, but their support was split because they wanted to be both democratic and progressive but also non-nationalistic, and secular rather than religious.

That didn't sit well in Slovakia.

The VPN were constantly dancing on a knife edge: putting communists on the candidate list but leaving Communism behind; talking about Slovakia, but not in a nationalist way; talking about freedom of religion but not being behind the church.

It was a complex challenge. Particularly as the movement's own structures were weak. They had members all around Slovakia but no way of finding out about them or how they saw their politics or even their nationality. There was no mechanism to find out, record, or respond to such information. Yet VPN success depended on this disparate group campaigning together. At regional meetings, the leadership had absolutely no control over what local leaders might say. There were no central directives. There was no party line that everyone had to stick to.

At Frank's urging, the VPN leadership decided to write a program that everybody, every member of the movement, could read so they could understand what it stood for.

Frank advised less on the content of the message than on how it was delivered. VPN had to develop a complex political program to be credible. But it also had to reduce that message to a series of short slogans on leaflets and posters that people could remember. Martin Šimečka took responsibility for writing the longer version, which Frank helped distill into a five-page synopsis from which the election slogans came.

Šimečka mined the United Nations Declaration of Human Rights, but the central question the program needed to address was the ongoing relationship between Czechs and Slovaks. The old constitution wouldn't work, because the Slovaks felt overlooked, so something new was required. But VPN didn't know what it was. They didn't know how they could answer the question. All they could say was "We want to create equal federal republics of Slovaks and Czechs in one state."

Any more detail would have been messy.

The program also considered human rights, what schools should teach, and the suitability of public bodies for freedom and democracy. VPN also tried to balance the right of private property and organize a new economy but the Slovaks weren't like the Czechs. The Czechs embraced capitalism. The Slovaks were far more wary.

RAISING THE PROFILE

If the elections had been held in January, VPN would have won easily. But they understood that they had to give other parties the chance to make their case. It was only fair.

Every party running in the elections was allocated an hour of TV advertising. So the TV became full of short videos day after day, and the same people who loved collecting the caricature cards watched the ads like crazy. People loved it. It was the first time, the first election. People loved the whole rigmarole.

VPN's videos were put together by Anton Mrazek, Andrew Frank's host. Mrazek worked in Slovak television, so he was a natural choice to produce the ads. They were the most professional in terms of their production values. Many of the videos from other campaigns simply had no production values. They were terrible. But the audience loved the whole experience because it was like a competition to make the best videos. They watched the political ads as if they were real programs. It was fantastic fun.

One way the Americans suggested to raise the profile of VPN, and of Slovakia in general, was by bringing the most famous living Slovak to the United States. Alexander Dubček, one of Frank's neighbors on the hill overlooking downtown Bratislava, was a hero among pro-democracy activists, and in the democratic West, for his attempt to reform Soviet communism during the Prague Spring of 1968, when he had lifted censorship and other restrictions under the slogan, "Socialism with a human face." Dubček had been forced from office when the Warsaw Pact invaded Czechoslovakia to end the Prague Spring and had spent the intervening decades in internal exile. Only after the Velvet Revolution of 1989, had he been brought back from obscurity to become chairman of the federal Czechoslovak government, a largely ceremonial position.

Volunteers for Democracy decided to bring him to the United States.

Andrew Frank went with Juraj to meet Dubček at his home on the hill in Bratislava, near the Mrazeks' house. The door was opened by an older man with thinning white hair, a dog at his slippered feet, and a blue cardigan sweater covering a rather frail body that looked its seventy-plus years.

The first time Frank had come across Dubček's name had been in his history books at school. The changes Dubček had tried to put forth, what he termed "socialism with a human face," scared Moscow into taking him and others from Prague and sending in tanks to quell the remarkable Prague Spring of

1968. The story resonated with Frank's own family's past in central Europe, and his fascination only grew from studying European history at college.

Now, on April 16, 1990, Juraj introduced Frank to Dubček as the American representative of the group that would be sponsoring and putting together his upcoming visit to Washington. The young American had put on a tie—very subdued for his taste—with a blue blazer and nice pants.

For twenty-two years Dubček had lived in relative obscurity, spending most of his years at the forestry ministry, but now he was rejuvenated. It was like seeing something powerful reach a peak. His frail body and his lack of English didn't bother Frank's image of a man who had tried to be the Gorbachev of his time but failed. Indeed, Dubček's kindly manner only increased Frank's admiration. There was something about the grandfatherly figure to which he felt a great kinship; he hoped the feeling was mutual.

It was clear that Dubček was in a relatively happy place. Frank understood that he'd had a rough go of it for a period, but now he seemed not just contented but also relieved. It struck the younger man how well the former leader had retained his dignity during the twenty-five years or more he was out of favor. Dubček seemed to feel a sense of personal relief that the fall of the Berlin Wall, the popular demonstrations, and the approaching elections would create opportunities for his fellow Slovaks. He wasn't ingrained in VPN's preparations for the elections, because his time was largely past, but he remained emblematic of the struggle so many people endured for the twenty years between the Prague Spring and the wall coming down.

The Slovaks viewed Dubček as not so much a hero as a symbol of the past that failed. Whatever he had tried to do, it failed. But they also recognized that he was a symbol for the west in a positive way. Volunteers for Democracy paid to bring him and Mihalik to the United States. The US consultants thought that Dubček's past would make him a powerful symbol of what was happening in Slovakia in particular and Eastern Europe in general.

Dubček got a warm welcome. The Prague Spring had been a big deal for US politicians bitterly opposed to Soviet influence. They were happy to fete its figurehead.

CHAPTER 7

AFTERMATH

FOUR DAYS BEFORE THE JUNE ELECTION, FRANK HAD another encounter with Dubček. This time, he was impressed not so much with the human qualities of someone who was clearly a deeply caring individual as with Dubček's abilities as a tough-minded politician. It was like an echo of his storied past.

Václav Havel made a trip to Slovakia to visit four cities and give speeches in support of the Civic Forum and VPN. The first stop was Komárno, a largely Hungarian city, followed by the traditional Slovak town of Nitra and then Bratislava. It was late afternoon when the motorcade pulled up at the site of the rally and all of the dignitaries and their entourage exited newly shined, chauffeur-driven Tatra automobiles.

The original plan was to stop at a coffee shop before heading out to greet the crowd, but the vehicles had pulled up about twenty minutes late and the large crowd was getting antsy. What to do: coffee or no coffee? The leaders were also alerted that a large contingent of Slovak nationalists had positioned themselves in front of the rally, near the podium. That spelled possible trouble.

Calmly, Dubček and an aide decided that coffee was in order, so they sat down and went over the program again, unperturbed by the tension outside. Then the entourage made its way toward the stage. Anybody who was anybody was there on the podium facing a huge, noisy crowd of some 60,000 people. For Frank, it was a remarkable sight at the end of a remarkable day, though he could not help regretting the prominence of the small but vocal section of Nationalists at the front.

The nationalists were highly savvy and well-organized. Most observers agreed that their leading members and their main control came from the Communist Party, so they had the potential to cause trouble in the region. The Slovak National Party leader had been the head of the police under the communist regime.

The first speaker was Milan Kňažko. His voice was eloquent and strong, and well-known to the crowd as one of the two main voices of the November Revolution in Bratislava. He opened with his standard, much loved, catchphrase: "Milli priatelia"—"Dear Friends." Some jeers were heard and then the Nationalists got louder. The crowd fired back. It was a bit scary because it looked like it could become angry. Some signs were torn and restlessness began to grow among the massive crowd of supporters who were clearly dismayed and annoyed with the small group of insurgents.

As disorder threatened to escalate, there came a bellow from the podium. A berating was taking place. "You are not schoolchildren," the voice said. "We have fought for democracy but not anarchy—and we will not stand for anarchy."

Dubček had seized the microphone. His performance was later described as a throwback to his greatest days. Never had people seen this side of the man. Until now, most people had not realized that this man who had once tried to lead them was still a force. The crowd listened. They quieted. The rally roared on with cheers. The Nationalists were defeated.

It was at that moment Frank knew the Nationalists would not have such a strong showing in the polls as many observers predicted, but they could have a future.

Dubček had spoken. He had set the tone. He had fought for democracy that day, maybe more so than on any other, or maybe he was fighting for his piece of the action in a time of still unsettled waters. Havel followed with a long and eloquent speech read through his bifocals to the now quieter but happy crowd. From jeers to cheers to election victory and a new beginning.

It was a day that would stay with Frank forever. The crowd cheered. Flags flew. Spontaneous demonstrations happened. Planned demonstrations heated up. Confrontations manifested. The election was getting close. The people felt it, and Frank felt it.

It was nothing like anything anyone could appreciate unless they had stood in front of a crowd of 60,000 cheering people and seen their faces. Everyone was happy, and some were crying with happiness. Apart from the silenced Nationalists, of course.

This election was special and everyone knew it. Frank was increasingly confident of a VPN victory. They had the momentum behind them.

Four days later, on election day, Frank was present when Dubček arrived at a polling station in an old school to cast his vote. The American was accompanied by the photographer from *Details* magazine, who thought it would be a good idea to capture a handshake between Frank and the elder statesman when Dubček arrived. Frank did not. He was excited to see Dubček again after a little while and on such a momentous day. But that was enough in itself. It wasn't his style to have the meeting photographed (although he had to admit to being somewhat flattered by the idea of being tailed by a reporter and photographer).

Frank waited near the booth that people used to pick their selections with yet more photographers waiting for Dubček to arrive. There was some general excitement when someone shouted that he had arrived, and everyone started checking their cameras. It turned out to be a case of mistaken identity, as the man who entered the room with his short, meek wife was not Dubček but Josef Bilak, the former communist ideologue. Perhaps all the former political generations looked the same.

The Bilaks went to the booth and deposited the envelopes with their ballots. A reporter asked Bilak how he had enjoyed voting in a free election. Bilak pointed out that he had voted freely many times. When he was asked the last time, he replied, "The last? Oh yes, 1946."

For Frank, it was the single quote that summed up the remarkable nature of what was happening, but he noticed it was not picked up by any of the major American publications. They were too busy in Prague.

Moments later, Dubček arrived—the real Dubček—and went into the booth to pick his ballots. He looked up and recognized Frank, looked down, looked up again, and smiled and said "Hello" as he stuffed his envelope. At that moment, Frank felt more strongly than ever that the older man was like his grandfather, with a sparkle in his eyes.

A few seconds later, as Dubček walked to the box to deposit his ballots, he paused for the cameras. Just long enough for an American election observer to reinforce European stereotypes of pushy Americans. She jumped toward the box and shouted at her fellow observer, "Take my picture, take my picture."

In all his time on the C&E tour and working with VPN, Frank had never felt the need to be rude. The idea that someone would behave in such a crass manner toward someone like Dubček was greatly upsetting. This was a day for celebration, not for embarrassment.

In the end, well over 80 percent of Slovaks went to the polls, and VPN got 30 percent of the vote. It made them the winners. The Christian Democrats came second with 19 percent, followed by the former communists with 14 percent and the nationalists with 10 percent.

It was a victory, but it paled in comparison with the achievement of VPN's sister party in Prague, where Civic Forum got 60 percent. It was clear that Slovakia was already becoming a different country from the Czech Republic. Although VPN had ended up with a mandate in Slovakia, it was a far smaller one.

SELF HARM

Almost at once things began to fall apart.

The biggest threat to the VPN turned out not to come from the Christian Democrats or from the former communists—but from within their own ranks.

It was an open secret in Slovakia that tens of thousands of people had acted as agents of the secret police, including a lot of ordinary people who reported on their friends and neighbors. As part of its desire to break with the past, VPN had announced that anyone who had signed a contract with the secret police would not be allowed to take part in the elections. If their involvement came to light after the elections, they would lose their position and not be involved with the VPN.

Two days before the election, they learned that Ján Budaj had been an agent of the secret service.

Not only had Budaj become the leader of the party, thanks to his dynamic public appearances and widespread popularity for over a decade. He had been a close friend of the other dissidents. Learning that he had betrayed them was a devastating psychological and emotional blow.

It was too close to the elections to take Budaj off the ballot, but after their victory, the leaders of the VPN forced him to resign.

An emotional Budaj went into hiding. He never forgave his former colleagues.

It was confusing for the Slovak electorate, at least some of whom had cast their votes on the strength of Budaj's appeal. It was particularly bewildering for VPN, who found themselves having to make many decisions and moral compromises. One of them was to cut loose their friend. Šimečka and the others argued that they had no choice.

On the other hand, VPN had achieved so much. For many of them, it was like a miracle. After years of railing against the communists, they finally had their own government. Still, none of them anticipated the world of pain it would take to create a government and find a prime minister after Budaj's fall from grace.

Even the parties who ended up going into opposition benefited from having taken part in the elections. They had established their voice in the government. Only the nationalists were not happy. The 10 percent of voters who supported them were not satisfied with the result at all. They were starting to call more openly for an independent Slovak state. In the end, their dissatisfaction would lead to the end of Czechoslovakia.

As VPN celebrated its victory, Andrew Frank was struck by how far VPN had come in the short period since the Velvet Revolution. For Martin Šimečka, however, the victory was already bittersweet.

In his mind, dark forces were starting to emerge in Slovak society. He saw the future—and it scared him. The craziness that had been kept hidden in communist times was suddenly back.

The toppling of Ján Budaj led to a few weeks of uncertainty and infighting. Ultimately, it allowed Vladimír Mečiar, a former communist who had been a minister in the interim government, to become leader of VPN and the first prime minister of Slovakia. Mechiar's political instincts lent toward the autocratic and the nationalist.

He took VPN in a new direction.

INDEPENDENCE

Slovak independence from the Czech Republic came four years later, inspired largely by Mechiar, who had remained in power that entire time. Whether things would have been different if Budaj had taken power is not clear.

Many people in VPN were very close to Václav Havel and Civic Forum, who believed in putting a unified, strong Czechoslovakia in the heart of Europe. But many other Slovaks resented what they saw as the prejudice shown toward them by their Czech neighbors. Frank noticed that when he went with some of the VPN to Prague to get visas to visit the United States, even the way the officials spoke to them at the window was patronizing and insulting. The Czechs looked down on the people in Slovakia. Many Slovaks saw the Czechs as their brothers and sisters, but the sentiment was not reciprocated.

Perhaps independence was inevitable.

As for the other leaders of the VPN, they soon fell out. Martin Šimečka went into journalism. Juraj Mihalik wrote a book called *Velvet Failures* that presented a particularly bitter view of his former colleagues. Ján Budaj was somewhat disgraced for a while but clawed his way back into politics without ever again becoming a major figure.

US PRESENCE

The changes in Eastern Europe led to a huge expansion in the activity and reputation of American political consultants. Carl Gershman, president of the National Endowment for Democracy (NED), happened to be in Bratislava on his way elsewhere, the day the group arrived. Gersham was upset that C&E was doing the NED's job. In fact, he discussed this point with James Dwinell, stating that the NED's brief was to help fund the International Republican Institute and the National Democratic Institute and such election support programs. He was not happy at all with the involvement of a private company.

In fact, the involvement of private consultants was to become far more common in the very near future. The *Campaigns & Elections* group were not the first political consultants to head to Eastern Europe in the late 1980s after the wall came down, and they certainly weren't the last. The nineties really opened the door for political consultants to go around the world. Under the Clinton administration, people who ultimately became big names began to work abroad, such as James Carville and Stan Greenberg, who helped Tony Blair become elected prime minister in the United Kingdom in 1997. Many went on to work in Israel. The fashion continued in the early 2000s.

Since the Trump presidency, and particularly the election of December 2020, American politics has taken something of a battering. Today, it might be worth calling overseas political consultants to advise the Americans.

SEPARATE WAYS

Volunteers for Democracy did not become part of the international consultancy vogue. They looked briefly at the next frontier for democracy, which was Russia, but things never came together, and they all went back to their lives.

It wasn't so much that they missed the boat. It was more that the boat didn't seem to be going anywhere particularly interesting after the trip they'd just finished.

James Dwinell, meanwhile, was so pleased with the whole tour to Eastern Europe that he quickly set up another later that year in the former Soviet Union. Andrew Frank helped Dwinell set up venues in Moscow, Leningrad, and Kiev. He found his welcome less warm than it had been in Bratislava.

In Moscow, he was kicked out of his hotel at one in the morning because the secret police were eavesdropping on his phone and took objection to the fact that he was promoting democracy. They left him on the street with his bag, trying to figure out where he could sleep. He persevered, however, and eventually managed to set up a conference with hundreds of attendees.

Dwinell, on the other hand, was so pleased with the Russia trip he ended up marrying his interpreter.

Kelly Kimball vowed never to get involved in international politics again. Not because the result had gone wrong, but because at the time it was not yet clear that it had. He'd already reached the peak of his career. Politics could not get any better. How many thirty-year-olds get to say they got involved in something that actually helped change a map?

The chance to have worked outside of the United States was fantastic. Kimball was used to dealing with people who were born and bred to be in politics, who didn't give a hoot about anything beyond a few core issues. On his tour through former Communist countries, he met a group of people who would go to prison rather than let anyone tell them what to say. For a young political junkie in the United States, it was one of the most energetic and enlightening situations he could ever imagine.

And now he was done. The trip marked the beginning of the end of his involvement in politics.

Not discouraged by his attempts to ship computers to Slovakia, Kimball focused his career on founding technology companies as the Internet grew in popularity.

But he never forgot the thrill of sitting in front of people who would actually respond to his suggestions by saying, "Yes, we'll do that. That's how we're going to win this election." It was one of the most direct experiences a political operative could have: saying something and watching it be put into action.

He was proud that the Volunteers for Democracy had been part of the success of the VPN. But a few years later, when the country decided to split, he found himself wondering, "My God, did we do that?"

That remains the overriding emotion today, more than three decades later. "Oh, my God!" Today, Slovakia is officially considered a flawed democracy, like the Czech Republic, Poland, Hungary—and the United States. It is peaceful and prosperous. It holds the record for turning out more automobiles per head than any other country in the world.

The generation of politicians that brought about the Velvet Revolution have largely died or have drifted out of politics. Some are happy with what they achieved, while others, like Martin Šimečka, are more ambivalent in their views.

But for Fadem, Frank, Kimball, and Whitcomb, whose very trip to Eastern Europe was fired by their dedication to the democratic process, one consideration ranks higher than all others. Whatever happened in Slovakia was the choice of the Slovaks, and no one else. That's the nature of democracy.

Even if its workings remain at heart a mystery.

AFTERWORD

KELLY KIMBALL

We are all going to have a conversation with ourselves—the single most important of our lives. At the end of our time here, at that last flash of consciousness, money will mean nothing. Even time will have no value. The only thing that will matter in that moment will be that final conversation when we look back on our lives and ask ourselves "Did I live a fearless life? Could I have impacted the world had I only had the courage to act?"

I hadn't had these thoughts when we embarked on our road trip. The thought that this would be something other than another interesting adventure had never entered my mind. The truth is, that single two-week period changed my entire life. I realized that we all have the power to make a difference. All we have to have is the courage to take the leap. That message was so profound that I took many subsequent "road trips." I started new companies—significant companies—that have had profound impacts on our markets. This has led me to a life of mentoring, teaching, investing, and charity—all with an understanding that these efforts, no matter how small, can change the world.

None of this would have been possible without these two transformative weeks. Our little road trip became the most powerful, impactful, and important two weeks of my life.

For that, I will be forever grateful.

TRISH WHITCOMB

I grew up in a political family and, by the time I traveled to Eastern Europe, had worked professionally in more than thirty campaigns. By the time I stepped on the plane in Frankfurt for Budapest, I had seen John and Robert Kennedy, and civil rights leader Martin Luther King, Jr., slain. My contemporaries fought and died in what I thought was a purposeless war in Southeast Asia. Fashion and music—miniskirts, the British Invasion, bikinis, and the Beach Boys—provided much-needed solace. I had heard of "Prague Spring," but was too deep into the "Summer of Love" at Woodstock to pay much attention.

The trip we took to former Eastern Bloc countries changed me in ways I never imagined. It rekindled my faith in the collective action of passionate individuals demanding change. It also showed me how, in the long run, divisively branding fellow citizens as "others" shattered the bonds required to keep democratic principles at the forefront of politics and policy.

I had the privilege of meeting former political prisoners-turned-activists striving to make Democracy work in former communist countries. Those events sharpened my awareness of the allure and fragility of democracy. Watching men and women who once fought for it in those countries in 1991 now subverting it is personal and painful. Seeing America's democracy inching toward authoritarianism is horrifying. People of the world deserve better.

BARRY FADEM

As Democracy is threatened on a daily basis in this country, writing this book provided a small oasis of hope for me. Even though our trip to Eastern Europe seemed so long ago, vivid memories came back—talking with real people with tears in their eyes because, at long last, they too could live in a Democracy.

Listening to the stories of persons who had been beaten, imprisoned, and deprived of all rights for as long as they could remember was gut-wrenching. But the joy they brought to the conversations because the People HAD won and they could now control their own destiny was breathtaking and overwhelming. It was an honor to meet all of these new "citizens of democracy" and it was incredibly fulfilling to actually help them in our small way.

We were all welcomed with open arms every place we went because we were seen as true representatives of Democracy and they viewed the "great United States" as the beacon of freedom. It saddens me to think how we would have been received in 2022. We need to restore this country's image in the eyes of the world. And yes, I intentionally capitalized "Democracy" and actually believe it should be in all Caps—DEMOCRACY. For all of the millions of people living in Eastern Europe, DEMOCRACY was an impossible dream that was fulfilled. So, I will always have hope.

ANDREW FRANK

"Berlin Wall Falls" and "Florio Wins Big" were the two headlines I was pondering in early November 1989. I had just come off a winning gubernatorial campaign in New Jersey, but the pull of Eastern Europe was fascinating in a different way than Trenton had been. I had no idea what I was getting into, pre-cell phones and pre-Internet, but it turned out to be the journey of a lifetime.

The memories of 1990 in Eastern Europe and the people we met along the way show that change is indeed possible. It's a matter of what people do with change that facilitates positive impact.

I have a brick from the Berlin Wall on my desk and look at it almost every day—seeing the possibilities. Democracy is fragile, seemingly more so now than ever, and we as Americans tend to tell people how it should be: take the good from our system and try to recognize the bad to shape young democracies differently.

The creation of this book—which allowed the four of us to reconnect about a great time in our lives—comes at a time in which, globally, the concept of democracy is threatened. While I like to think we played a small part in the early stages of a few countries in Europe that led to the changes in others, we must continue to move forward and protect the institutions we have created. Stability and respect, when it comes to democracy, are all too fragile.

I hope you had a few laughs from our adventures but, more importantly, I hope you grasped the importance of some of our messages. When we examine the contemporary world, including the United States, it is clear that it's vital to continue the ongoing work of protecting the freedoms and choices of the people.

ACKNOWLEDGMENTS

KELLY KIMBALL

After years of regaling my sons with tales of our Eastern European trip, my eldest, Ryan, reminded me that none of the stories I had told them could be Googled. After months of trying to convince myself that I needed to write all this down, I finally relented. Thank you to my family—Carla, Ryan, and Brady—for convincing me to start this process. If it weren't for you three nothing in my life would be possible. A very special thank you to Trish, Barry, and Andrew. The hours and hours of conversations about the trip always ended up with us laughing hysterically. Thank you for making this one of the more memorable projects I have ever embarked upon. And finally, words cannot express our gratitude for the one and only Tim Cooke—our writer—who suffered through two years of our craziness!

TRISH WHITCOMB

Many thanks to Kelly Kimball and our fellow travelers, Barry Fadem, Andrew Frank, and our scribe, Tim Cooke, for a journey back to a seminal series of events in our lives and the lives of people we met on our trip. Sometimes it is easy to forget that democracy is constantly a work in progress. It is impossible to forget the people who hold democracy dear, wherever they live and however they continue the fight.

BARRY FADEM

I want to thank Deb for our wonderful journey together and the inspiration she has always provided. And then I want to thank every person that I met on our "revolution road trip" for allowing me to watch true DEMOCRACY at work.

ANDREW FRANK

When my wife and I were dating, I went to Haiti. Her friend yelled in the background, "Break up with him! He's in the CIA!" My daughters didn't believe me about some of the adventures I told them about. This book is so they all know a little something more about me and an adventure I will never forget. I couldn't have done this journey without Tami, Tehya, and Maya. And a big thank you to Kelly for bringing us all together!

And finally, thank you from all of us to Jennifer Lazlo Mizrahi, Scott Berkowitz, James Dwinell, Phil Noble, James Noble, Greg Lyle, and Martin Šimečka for speaking to us and helping us recall some of these adventures. Thank you too, to Gordon and Mary Robson, for sharing their photos and other memorabilia, which also helped to inspire us.

Made in the USA
Coppell, TX
18 May 2023

17004022R00104